A Woman
in a Man's World

A Woman in a Man's World

Thérèse F. Casgrain

Translated by Joyce Marshall
Foreword by Frank R. Scott

McClelland and Stewart Limited

ISBN   0-7710-1915-7

The Canadian Publishers
McClelland and Stewart Limited
25 Hollinger Road, Toronto 374

The author wishes to thank the Canada Council for their grant toward the publication of this book.

The author also wishes to thank Shirley Thompson, Marie-Claire Dion, Marguerite MacDonald, and Florence Martel for their invaluable assistance.

Printed and bound in Canada

To the memory of my husband whose love and wisdom have been a constant source of strength for me during my work in the field of human rights in Canada.

To my children, Rodolphe, Hélène, Paul, and Renée.

Contents

Foreword

When it was suggested that I might contribute a preface to this autobiography I was hesitant. It was an honour I appreciated, but what could I add to the story of Thérèse Casgrain? She was already a very well-known Canadian personality when I first met her. She has made for herself a unique career, which only she can record. She has innumerable friends, many of whom have known her longer than I have. When I put my doubts to her, she made one of her characteristic remarks; "Well, you and I are what Canada ought to be. We represent the two cultures, but we do not fight." There was nothing for me to do but accept.

Considering her background in the aristocracy of French Canada, so vividly described here, the subsequent evolution of her activities and interests is remarkable. She moved by a sure intuition, rather than by intellectual analysis, toward those movements in society which represented the new and progressive and away from the fixed and reactionary. The fight for women's political rights was but the first example of her dedication to human rights in general for men and children as well as for women. This led on to a deep concern over economic injustices and a break with the old political parties. Few who started where she did would have been able to face the unpopularity and frustrations that inevitably attended the life of an active member of the CCF in Quebec.

Other movements of reform and protest drew her. Consumers' rights, civil liberties, the struggle for peace—to these and other activities she gave of her seemingly inexhaustible energy and time. Through it all she kept her eyes fixed on a concept of Canada as a country where the two principal components, the French and the English, might evolve harmoniously in fruitful cooperation.

9

She believed in an "equal partnership" before there ever was a B & B Commission.

Not least remarkable is the fact – as all who know her will testify – that she showed it is possible for a woman to play an active role in public life without losing any of her personal charm or giving up any of her duties as wife and mother. In the same afternoon she would be on the picket line for striking workers and later at a social gathering in her own milieu where she would question employers about their labour policies. She was the most feminine of feminists, of whom a trade-unionist once said to me; "She makes every boy feel a man and every man feel a boy."

The Marxist-Leninists, the Maoists, and those who do not believe in the democratic process will doubtless dismiss this story as bourgeois and unprofitable. But those who know that continuous reform is essential and possible in our parliamentary system, will recognize that Thérèse Casgrain has made a great personal contribution to Canadian democracy.

FRANK R. SCOTT

I

In the Land of My Forefathers

The long history of my family, and that of my husband, probably explain the urge for reform I have felt for so long and my deep interest in public affairs. My own family, the Forgets, have been established in Canada since the middle of the seventeenth century, when Nicolas Forget or Froget, also known as Despatis, of Normandy, arrived in the Montreal district. His descendants settled for the most part in Terrebonne, Repentigny, Lachenaye, and Saint-François on Île Jésus. In Terrebonne a Forget still works a farm known as *la Terre de chez nous*, which has belonged to the family for almost two centuries.

Nicolas' first wife was Madeleine Martin, the daughter of Abraham Martin, called "the Scotsman," who bequeathed his name to the battlefield where the armies of Wolfe and Montcalm met in 1759–the Plains of Abraham.[1] Later members of my family fought in the political uprising of 1837. The French-Canadian historian, Senator L.O. David, tells in *Les Patriotes de 1837-8* that Charles, Étienne, and Jean-Baptiste Forget of Saint-Janvier in Terrebonne County went to Saint-Eustache to join Chénier.

My father was born in Terrebonne on the 10th of December, 1861: his father, David-Rodolphe Forget, was a lawyer, and his mother, Angèle Limoges, the half-sister of the Honourable L.O. Taillon, who became prime minister of the province of Quebec in 1892. The only son in a family of four, he had just started his classical studies at *Collège Masson* in Terrebonne when the school was destroyed by fire. His uncle, Senator Forget, who was head of a brokerage house in Montreal and had only daughters, then sent for him with a view to some day taking him into the firm. At the age of fourteen, my father entered his uncle's office where one of his first duties, it seems, was polishing the brass plate on the outside of the building. While learning the mysteries of finance during the day–and a working day was exceedingly long then–he continued his studies in the evening. He thus learned the value of education the hard way and throughout his life he was anxious to help all those who wanted to improve themselves.

My maternal ancestors came to Canada at almost the same time as the Forgets. In 1651 François Blondeau was living in Quebec City on Chemin Sainte-Foy. He subsequently acquired a farm on Grande-Allée and settled definitely, a few years later, in Charlesbourg with his wife, Nicole Roland d'Assonville, also known as Gabrielle d'Assonville. There is some mystery about the origins of this young lady. On one hand, the marriage registry of the church shows that she was from the parish of Saint-Sulpice in Paris but, on the other, she declared before a notary in her marriage contract that she was the daughter of the late Pierre Roland, the governor of Luxin in Lorraine.[2]

François Blondeau and his wife settled first in Quebec City and there their ten children were born. One of their sons became a captain in the militia and later *seigneur* of Rivière-du-Loup.[3] The story goes that he became so involved in the life of the community that one of his children had a Malecite Indian as godfather. The Blondeau line spread throughout the region and for the next hundred years prospered in farming or trade.

Once again the Rebellion of 1837 touches the story of my family. After the defeats of Saint-Charles, Saint-Denis, Saint-Eustache, and Saint-Benoît, the proclamation of martial law, and the deportation of several prisoners, there was a period of calm. But in November 1838, new acts of violence erupted simultaneously in several places: at Beauharnois, rebels even seized the arms depot. It is easy to imagine the alarm of the inhabitants of this town, most of them peaceful citizens without political bias and dreading the vengeance of the English soldiers who, they felt, were quite capable of burning their village as they had Saint-Eustache and Saint-Benoît the year before. The heads of families left their work and rushed home to barricade their doors and windows: express orders had been given to close the *volets*, those heavy pine shutters still to be found on old houses built in the French-Canadian style.

One of the girls of the parish, Archange Quevillon, did not choose to obey. So through her wide-open window she caught sight of a battalion of Highlanders, marching proudly along in their tartan kilts and fur bonnets with chinstraps. During a short halt one of the soldiers approached the house to ask the pretty young girl for a drink and it was love at first sight for both of them. But their romance, like all true love-stories, was not without its trials. If we are to believe the story as it has come down to us, the tragic events they were caught up in almost parted them forever, for the handsome young Scot was taken prisoner. But when the rebels learned of the defeat of their comrades at Odell-town, they released their captives and James MacDonald hastened to his beloved. However, the girl's parents were far from approving the match. Her father, Jean-Maurice Quevillon, belonged to a family of artists, wood-sculptors, and patriots. He thought it quite unsuitable to give his daughter in marriage to one of those redcoats who so recently had been considered enemies. Two years passed with weighing the pros and cons of the union but the girl held out and finally won the day. Thanks to the favourable intervention of an uncle, Abbé Joseph Quevillon, *curé* of Saint-Polycarpe, the marriage was celebrated in Saint-Clément Church in Beauharnois on the 2nd of March, 1840. Those young lovers were my great-grandparents.

The economic prosperity brought to the Rivière-du-Loup region by the Intercolonial Railway encouraged the MacDonalds to settle there. In this part of the country lived the already thriving Blondeau family, and in 1866 my grandfather, Rodrigue MacDonald, then aged twenty, married Marie Blondeau, daughter of Antoine Blondeau and Angèle Lebel of Sainte-Anne-de-le-Pocatière. Thus the vigorous blood of the Scottish race was blended once again with that of the French. My mother, Blanche MacDonald, one of the children of this marriage, spoke only French in her childhood, but several years at the Convent of Mount St. Vincent in Halifax gave her a knowledge of English that did credit to her name.

My husband's ancestors came to Canada about a hundred years after the Forgets and the Blondeaus. Jean-Baptiste Casgrain, the first to settle here, had enlisted in the army while very young and had known the miseries of military campaigns in various parts of Europe and even in Turkey. He finally set sail for Canada in 1750, where he acquired property in Quebec City, on rue Sous-le-Fort in the Lower Town, a spot which still attracts so many visitors by its charm. There he kept a hostelry called *La Cloche bleue*, which quickly enabled him to make his fortune. He married Marguerite Cazeau, and in 1791 moved to Rivière-Ouelle with his by then numerous family. His eldest son, Pierre, bought the *Seigneurie de la Bouteillerie* and married Marie Bonenfant, by whom he had thirteen children. With his help the village built a convent and the first bridge over the Rivière Ouelle. In 1830, one of his sons, Charles-Eusèbe, became the member for Kamouraska in the Quebec Legislative Assembly. Later, he was on the special council appointed by Lord Durham to draw up a new constitution to replace the one that had been suspended by an act of the British parliament in February 1837. During the troubles in that same year, he did his utmost to maintain calm and support the government's efforts to restore peace.

Upon his death, Pierre Casgrain was buried beneath his seigneurial pew in the church at Rivière-Ouelle, and his eldest son, Pierre-Thomas Casgrain, succeeded him as seigneur. François, my husband's grandfather, and the son of Pierre-Thomas, died at the age of thirty-two, leaving his wife, the former Georgina Morison, with seven young children. The eldest, another François, my husband's father, studied medicine and set up practice in Montreal, where he married Adèle Berthelot, the daughter of Mr. Justice Joseph-Amable Berthelot. Of the three children of this marriage only my husband survived.

Charles Berthelot, my husband's maternal ancestor, came to Quebec as a tourist in the autumn of 1726. He intended to see New France and study trade, but also fell in love with pretty Thérèse Roussel, the daughter of the surgeon, Timothée Roussel. As Charles was a minor, he had to wait a year for permission to come from his father in France before he could marry. From this union resulted eleven children. In 1758, just before setting out on a return visit to France, he named his wife his "general and special proxy" for the duration of his projected trip–a trip from which he never returned, since the conquest of New France intervened. His great-grandson, who was born in Montreal in 1815, was Joseph-Amable Berthelot, my husband's maternal grandfather. He articled with Sir Louis-Hippolyte Lafontaine and became his associate after being admitted to the bar on the 12th of November 1836. Soon afterwards the troubles of 1837 began. Though a patriot, he was never in favour of armed revolt. Even so, in November 1838 he was thrown into prison with many others as peace-loving as himself. After several days' detention, he wrote to the secretary of Sir John Colborne asking the reason for his arrest. There was no answer to his letter but he was released a week later.

In 1849 he married Julie McEnis, the adopted daughter of Mr. Justice Elzéar Bédard. The latter had made a home for Julie and her sister after their parents died on the ship that was bringing them from Ireland to Quebec.

When Sir Louis-Hippolyte Lafontaine was appointed to the bench in 1853, Amable Berthelot formed a new partnership with his friend, Sir Georges-Étienne Cartier. On the 30th of November, 1860, he was appointed judge of the Superior Court for the district of Montreal. He spent many holidays in France and his daughter Adèle, my husband's mother, writes in her journal of a visit he made in 1872 to the famous chemist Berthelot, his distant cousin. I have in my possession several letters to Amable Berthelot from Sir Louis-Hippolyte Lafontaine and Sir Georges-Étienne Cartier, as well as from the lawyer Joseph Doutre who became so notorious during the famous Guibord trial.

Like many other women, those of the families I have mentioned played an important social and political role from the earliest days of the colony. They made a valuable economic contribution in an era when farming, small family industries, and handicrafts were profitable occupations. To illustrate their importance in rural society of the time, here is a quotation from Léon Gérin of the Royal Society of Canada:

Madame C . . . is an energetic and accomplished woman. She seems to occupy a position in the family that is almost equal to that of the father. The domestic cares and the management of the home are her special charge. Better educated than her husband, she is responsible for family correspondence and takes an important part in the education of her children; she presides over family devotions and leads the prayers.

She may sometimes not sit at the table while the men are eating but this is because there are no servants and also because the table is small: she does not consider herself inferior to her husband. By virtue of her marriage contract, the goods she brought as dowry or that have accrued to her since her marriage remain her own.

She co-operated with her husband in drawing up their wills and, should she survive him, comes into possession of half the goods accumulated during the marriage through her own and her husband's labours. She would also acquire full enjoyment during her lifetime (or until her remarriage) of the share left by her husband. Significantly, her husband seldom fails to consult her before concluding the smallest purchase.[4]

A little later Léon Gérin states that the management of our early Canadian families differed slightly from that of our ancestors in France and explains the reason as follows:

Immense, unoccupied expanses of territory originally supplied the raw materials for two large industries that were based on the simple harvesting of natural products: first, the fur trade in which, from the beginnings of the French colony, the whole population was active at least to some extent; and then logging which became more and more important especially after the early years of the nineteenth century. These primitive industries, which were carried on over vast spaces and at great distances from the established farming communities, kept the heads of the families in the new parishes far from their homes for long periods. All this time the mother of the family was responsible not only for managing the household but also for seeing that the farm work was carried out. Her position thus became increasingly important.[5]

Her influence was felt not only in the homes but in the parishes and in the general community. Caring for the sick, assisting poor families and helping neighbours all received attention. During the first half of the nineteenth century this influence even extended to politics. After the country was divided in 1791 into two provinces – Lower Canada (Quebec) and Upper Canada (Ontario) – the parliament of each province included an executive council and a legislative council appointed by the king, as well as a legislative assembly elected by the people. The conditions required to be an elector were much like those of today. And, it should be noted, the law at that time made *no sex distinction*. The anti-feminists I encountered during my fourteen-year struggle to obtain the right to vote would have been greatly astonished to learn this historical fact.

The charitable activity of our women was particularly necessary during the frequent epidemics that ravaged Quebec. They helped set up emergency shelters in which the sick were crowded and took care of the orphans, who could be counted in the thousands. French and English-Canadian women worked side by side and devoted themselves to the care of the poor and the sick. To raise the funds necessary for their work, they organized the first bazaars, which were sometimes held in such fashionable places as the Masonic Hall in 1829, and the Rasco Hotel in 1842. Between 1842 and 1850 four religious communities of sisters were established in the Montreal diocese, and this somewhat changed the form of lay charity. In the Victorian era, the elegant ladies of the bourgeoisie, with their voluminous, flounced dresses of rustling taffeta and huge, frilled bonnets, made a strange constrast to the nuns, with their rough, greyish garments and white linen coifs. However, the fine lady was well aware that she would leave the hardest and the most unpleasant tasks to the sisters. Direct contact between the wealthy and the destitute, the charitable and those requiring charity, disappeared. The nun became the intermediary. Our lady patronesses, who were often too busy with social activities, gradually lost the habit of mingling with the lower strata of society, and thus social differences became more clearly defined.

Under sometimes very difficult conditions, our women have made a significant contribution to Canadian society. Over the last fifty or more years, I have been involved in the social and political events that marked my country and I can well understand the feelings of patriotism that slumber in the heart of every Quebecker. Yet, in spite of numerous reforms, Canadian women are still considered second-class citizens and they are too often deprived of the treatment and consideration they deserve as human beings. To try to rectify these wrongs became my goal.

II

Little Eloise

A charity performance in a theatre crowded with elegant ladies and gentlemen in evening dress, a curtain rising and falling before a series of *tableaux vivants* – this is one of my earliest memories. In the centre of the stage is a very little girl, myself, holding a Union Jack, who is supposed to sit perfectly still. But already I was of another mind and to the great amusement of the spectators I rose to wave at them and blow them kisses.

My father had built our house – which later became the *Cercle universitaire* – on Sherbrooke Street near Berri. At the time that part of the city was strictly residential. In the afternoons we children used to go for long drives in a little cart drawn by two ponies under the beautiful trees of Sherbrooke Street, which was paved then only as far as the *Collège de Montréal*, or along Western Avenue (now Boulevard de Maisonneuve), which was lined with lovely orchards, the property of the Décarie families. In spring nothing was prettier than all those apple trees in bloom. Cement and concrete have replaced that scene and the city has lost in charm and beauty what it has gained in modernity.

One day I was waiting at the door for the governess and my brothers to join me for our daily drive when the sight of a puddle gave me a mad desire to splash in it; I ran about in the water and got delightfully and completely wet, even my hair. There was no outing for me that day: I spent the afternoon doing penance.

A little later, I once again brought punishment down upon myself. What a scandal I caused by spitting from the top of the dumbwaiter on the head of one of the maids who didn't care particularly for the antics of a four-year-old and was always finding some way to get me scolded. When he learned that evening of what I had done, Papa gathered the household in the drawing-room and there, on my knees, I had to apologize to Félixine for insulting her. I have never forgotten that lesson on our duty to respect even those we do not love.

A gentle and submissive wife and an attentive mother, Maman was the model innocent young woman of her day. Tiny and pretty, she dressed with quiet but very certain taste, with a preference for a particular shade of deep blue that my father loved, for it matched her sparkling eyes. I can still see her in a dress of midnight-blue velvet that suited her to perfection. One day my parents were invited to a dinner-dance by Sir Montague and Lady Allan and Maman, delighted, prepared with pleasure for the party. At the last moment important business forced Papa—who wasn't very fond of social gatherings anyway—to beg off. A few days later Maman found a jewel-case holding a pearl necklace beside her place at the dinner table. This was my father's way of asking her forgiveness.

Since she had an excellent household staff, Maman was able to go out a great deal and to accompany my father when he travelled. Part of her free time was devoted to charitable activities. Women, especially those of the comfortable classes, enjoyed playing the role of lady bountiful and distributed food baskets in the homes of needy families every Christmas. They never dreamed, however, of trying to find out why these people were in need.

The style then was for long skirts and rustling petticoats with corsets to make waists as small as possible. Coiffures were elaborate, built up with hair-pieces know as *transformations*, and hats were enormous, if not monumental. Life was more ceremonious than today and gentlemen and ladies alike preferred evening dress for dining out and going to the theatre or to the homes of their friends.

Maman often gave what were called "five to seven o'clock musicals." Since cocktails weren't yet fashionable, ladies and gentlemen met to drink tea and nibble *petits fours* while listening to well-known performers. A certain baritone always thrilled the audience when he sang such romantic ballads of Chaminade as *L'Anneau d'argent* and *Au Pays bleu*.

Among our neighbours were Charles Hébert (who became Canadian Ambassador to Holland), his brother Jacques, and their two sisters, and Marcel Parizeau and his brother Gérard, whose son Jacques is well known today as an economist and politician.

Sir Olivier Taillon, my grandmother Forget's half-brother, was a regular visitor to our house. Highly active in the political affairs of both Quebec and Canada, he was prime minister of the province in 1887, leader of the opposition during the Mercier regime until 1890, a member of Boucherville's cabinet in 1892, and once again prime minister from 1892 to 1895. He impressed everyone with his personal integrity and vigorous opposition to political patronage and his administration was marked by a notable improvement in agriculture and the general economy of the province. At the federal level he served briefly as postmaster general in the government of Sir Charles Tupper just before the Conservatives were swept from power in 1896 by the Liberals under Laurier.

Although he had by then retired from active politics, my uncle still sometimes spoke on behalf of former colleagues. A childless widower, he boarded at the Deaf and Dumb Institute run by the Sisters of Providence. The ladies who also lived there and were still young at heart despite their white hair, could not hide their admiration for the handsome old man. At our house, we all considered his visits a treat; as I was still young, I was allowed to sit on his knee, and listen as he talked to my parents. His long, white beard so fascinated me that one day I had an impulse to braid it while he was carrying on a serious conversation with my father. I was promptly sent out of the room for that piece of daring.

On Epiphany he always entertained the family at a big dinner at the Viger, one of the elegant hotels of the day. Old and young delighted in these festivities and spirits were always high. Uncle Taillon had a beautiful voice and charmed us at Christmas and Easter when he sang *Adeste Fideles* or *Les Rameaux*. One of his contemporaries, Senator L. O. David, described him as follows: "(he was) ... physically strong and mentally brilliant combining the nature of a soldier with that of an artist, vital, animated, and many faceted .... Truly individual, he could change easily from abruptness and impatience to gentleness and tenderness. His brain was keen, and as brilliant as the aurora borealis, supple, and versatile; in his lively mind serious, even sombre, ideas and thoughts followed and replaced one another with the speed of lightning .... Full of life, his conversation was a rapid fire of witticisms, repartee, jokes, and humourous asides."[1]

From time to time, I would visit the deaf mutes' home. My grandmother also boarded there, as did Marine Lelland, today a well known professor and speaker, but then a little girl with whom I could play. She lived there with her mother, a pretty blonde woman, the typical Gibson girl. The nuns of the home had me act as godmother for ten-year-old Ludivine Lachance, who was deaf, mute, and blind and who had been brought there against the wishes of her parents. They had kept her in a sort of cage where she ate like a little animal and showed her joy or displeasure by grunts. With great patience the sisters had taught her enough so that she was able to recognize people by touch and to make her first communion. A sort of anguish always gripped me when she ran her hands over my face to see who I was. She lived to be eighteen years old, having known, thanks to the dedication of her teachers, something other than the solitude of a prisoner.

When I was eight years old, my parents sent me as a boarding-pupil to the convent of the Dames du Sacré-Coeur in Sault-aux-Récollets. Those were happy years for me although I was separated from my family from September until June. There was no question then of going home for weekends; we had to be satisfied with seeing our family in the parlour on Thursdays and Sundays and short vacations at Christmas and Easter. Among my school-mates were the daughters of Rodolphe Lemieux, Senator Belcourt, and Narcisse Dupuis. Corinne Dupuis, my rival in class and lifelong friend, later married Roger Maillet, the founder of *Le Petit Journal*; she herself edited the magazine *Amérique française* for many years and is a talented painter as well. Her fanciful exhibition of a few years ago, entitled *A la manière de* . . . , evoked with skill and humour the works of well-known artists.

One year my parents took me out of school to go with them on a trip to Paris, where my father had business. It was spring and Paris was magnificent; the chestnuts were in flower and on the Champs-Élysées, among the sumptuous carriages, a few automobiles could already be seen. We stayed at the Continental Hotel opposite the Tuilerie Gardens and, young as I was, I was taken to the Opéra and to the Opéra-Comique. As I was also fond of history, I enjoyed going to museums and looking at historical buildings and monuments with my French governess. One day my sister and one of her friends were invited by two young Canadians to spend an evening at Magic City, a big amusement park. These two Montreal students were later to achieve distinction, Georges Vanier as officer, ambassador, and Governor General of Canada, and Paul Morin as a poet, the author of *Paon d'émail*. At the last moment, my sister's friend fell ill and, as my parents did not want their daughter to go out alone with two young men, it was decided that I should accompany them. What an unexpected joy for me! I took advantage of all the rides and entertainments offered and particularly remember a slide with Georges Vanier that ended at the bottom of a large tub. Years later, at Rideau Hall, he jokingly reminded me of the evening when he took care of his friend's little sister. I can easily imagine the disappointment of the handsome young gentlemen when they found themselves obliged to take out a little convent-girl instead of a charming young lady their own age.

Our stay in Paris had to be prolonged because of my father's business, and so we narrowly missed the sinking of the *Titanic*, where our passage had already been booked. My mother was at Paquin's, a well-known couturier house, when news of the catastrophe arrived. The saleswomen ran excitedly through the salons, announcing the tragic news to the customers. That evening at the hotel my parents gave thanks to God for sparing them an almost certain death. Several of their acquaintances were, alas, among the victims.

More than anyone else, my father had a dominant influence on my life. He was a tall, slender man with an energetic and intelligent face. The somewhat severe expression of his grey-green eyes belied his great goodness and deep understanding. He could be very gay yet his presence commanded respect everywhere, but what characterized him above all was his enterprising spirit and dynamic personality. He was at once a Quebec nationalist and a conservative and his patriotism, while less dramatic than that of some of his ancestors of 1837, was none the less very sincere. This expressed itself in his determination to help his fellow Quebeckers and to improve their general living conditions. Towards this end, he laboured continually and his self-imposed discipline brought him while still very young to the summit of the financial world.

As soon as he had finished his education, my father joined the brokerage firm of his uncle, Louis-Joseph Forget. He handled matters so well during the latter's periodic absences that he had become a partner by the time he was twenty-six—a position he held until 1907, when he established his own brokerage house. The personalities of the two men complemented each other marvellously: my great-uncle was calm, well balanced, imperturbable, and cautious, whereas my father was quick, daring, energetic, and very sure of his opinions. L. J. Forget and Company was the most important brokerage house in Montreal, well known throughout Canada and even abroad.

In 1900 the Forget office brought about the merger of Montreal Gas and Royal Electric into a single firm, the Montreal Light, Heat and Power, a merger considered quite gigantic at that time. Several years later my father brought about other mergers—when several cotton mills joined to become Dominion Textiles and then, in 1910, when various companies in Quebec City merged to form the Quebec Railway, Light, Heat and Power Company, which controlled all the public services in the city: tramways, gas, and electricity.

Before World War 1, London was the chief source of investment capital for Canada. My father believed that it would be to the advantage of our country to diversify its means of financing by borrowing on the French *Bourse*. To facilitate this, he founded the *Banque Internationale*, which received its charter from the federal government shortly after Sir Robert Borden came to power. Besides serving on the boards of several nation-wide companies where no French Canadian had ever sat before, he played an important role, with Sir Max Aitken, in the transactions that merged Dominion Iron and Steel, Dominion Coal Company and the Canada Cement Company. "What Forget will cheerfully undertake in the stock market would make the average broker aghast."[2] So wrote one of the big financial papers of the times. He was one of the first French-speaking Canadians to put the lie to the dictum: "The English for finance, the French for oratory."

Mrs. Francoeur, who worked for many years at L. J. Forget

and Company and witnessed at first hand the events she describes in her book *Trente ans, rue Saint-François Xavier et ailleurs*, wrote of my father: "It was quite amusing and at the same time flattering to us to see this young man of between thirty and thirty-five – he was forty at the turn of the century – leading all his English colleagues around by the nose with their smart customers trailing behind them"[3] The uncle-nephew association had striking results, as these lines show: "Whatever one may choose to write or say of them now, the operations of Rodolphe Forget between 1882 and 1907, on an exchange that had scarcely twenty-five members at the beginning and not many more than forty when he left the parent firm, are still among the most extraordinary feats the Montreal Stock Exchange has ever known."[4] And again: "L. J. Forget was then the leading brokerage house in the Dominion and, except for high-level, outside influences, set the pace for the stock market."[5] Speaking of my great-uncle and my father and aware of the criticism they received, she wrote: "How could these two men, the first of their people to reach the summit of the financial world and the only ones who were ever able to impress the English, fail to arouse jealousy and envy?"[6] At this period, moreover, Canadian business was almost entirely controlled by Anglo-Saxon capital and it is easy to imagine the difficulties encountered by French-speaking Canadians who tried to play a role in the financial world.

Left a widow while very young, Mrs. Francoeur had an only son, Louis, a brilliant journalist whose remarkable radio program, *La Situation, ce soir*, had a wide following during World War II. Jacques Francoeur, present owner of the newspaper *Dimanche-Matin*, is his son.

I have often wondered where my interest in social problems originated. When I was still very young and the Montreal Light, Heat and Power Company was controlled in large part by L. J. Forget and Company, I heard a great deal of talk about labour unrest because of a threatened strike of the tramway workers. It was my father who settled this dispute, and his success here impressed me very much.

Yielding to pressure from all sides, my father decided that he could serve his people better by entering active politics. So in the federal election of 1904, he ran as Conservative candidate in Charlevoix against the Liberal, Charles Anger. In his election platform he promised to build a railway between Quebec City and La Malbaie. In those days most people in La Malbaie thought twice before undertaking the journey to the capital; by the road over the capes, it required relays of horses and took a full day. My father had noticed how isolated this picturesque area of the province became as soon as the shipping season ended. As long as the river was open, a special boat was put at the disposal of farmers, but in winter they had to take their produce to market in Quebec City over a rough road through the rocky capes, a distance of between sixty and ninety miles. My father wanted the existing rail-line from Quebec City to Saint-Joachim extended to La Malbaie, to serve the principal villages in Charlevoix County.[7]

After his victory in the election, he devoted himself to improving the living conditions of his constituents. His projects were vast and he saw far into the future. To him the Quebec-Saguenay Railway was only a beginning and he wished to continue the line along the north shore of the St. Lawrence through Labrador to Cap-Saint-Charles. From there, ocean-crossings would be much more direct and rapid than by the Liverpool-New York or Liverpool-Halifax route.

After his re-election in 1908, my father divided his time between parliament, Charlevoix County, and his business in Montreal. He built a model farm in Baie-Saint-Paul and, to improve the stock of the cattle and horses, made stud animals available without charge to the local farmer groups, and organized numerous competitions. Later at La Malbaie, he founded a pulp and paper mill, a thriving company known today as Donahue Brothers. While president of the Richelieu and Ontario Company, he built a hotel at Tadoussac to help develop tourism. A few years later, he built the famous Manoir Richelieu at La Malbaie (or Murray Bay), a vacation-spot known for the beauty of its setting. Father decided to build a summer home for his family a few miles away in Saint-Irénée, a charming village stretching from a wooded hill down to a long, white, sandy beach. Friends followed his example: Mr. Justice Joseph Lavergne and Sir Rodolphe Routhier also built summer houses there and a hotel was erected for the growing number of vacationers.

The little parish church with its pleasing lines still stands proudly above the river, which is about ten miles wide at this point. The view is really splendid. To the east the La Malbaie and Cap-à-l'Aigle headlands stretch out into the water. In this peaceful spot, lulled by the murmur of the waves and invigorated by the salt air and the scent of the evergreens, we spent unforgettable summers. Papa came to *Gil'mont*, as we named our summer home, as often as he could and took pleasure in making it ever more beautiful. This was probably also his way of providing work for the local people, who fished and farmed, eking out a bare existence with their tiny boats and plots of unproductive soil. He loved to talk to these people and used to invite them to the house. One day one of the local men, seeing Maman approach, exclaimed in admiration, "Lady Forget, you remind me of Queen Victoria in her Vatican!" (In rural Quebec at that time one often saw, hanging in a place of honour with the family portraits, pictures of those great ones of this world whom our people venerated: the Pope, Queen Victoria, and Sir Wilfrid Laurier.)

When my father visited his riding, he did not pass unnoticed, for he always mounted the abrupt incline leading to Pointe-au-Pic and La Malbaie in a break drawn by four horses. Later he travelled the barely passable roads and steep hills of Charlevoix in a red touring-car, the first automobile ever seen in the region. When it first appeared, this strange monster aroused either curiosity or terror, and as it passed by horses would rear and even the children would run away and hide. Nor did the American tourists look too kindly upon this fiery contraption that had come to disturb their peace and quiet. But for us every outing was a joyful event and, when we set off, the ladies suitably protected by veils and dust-coats, we felt that we were going on a real expedition.

For forty years Saint-Irénée had the same *curé*. The story goes that this excellent but somewhat taciturn priest, a native of Lake St. John, had begun to study law in Quebec City. He once confided to us that the Bishop of Chicoutimi had summoned him one day to persuade him that his duties lay in religion, where he could perform great services. Probably influenced by his mother, whose only son he was, he gave up law for the seminary. Later his natural bent for business reappeared and he opened a branch of the *Banque*

Provinciale in his rectory, right across from Ernest Tremblay's general store with its branch of the *Banque Canadienne Nationale*. Such amusing incidents were food for conversation and gossip in the villages.

Gil'Mont–my eldest brother's name was Gilles–was built near the river at the top of a maple-covered slope. The house and the various outbuildings were on different levels and connected by pathways or steps. The landscape architect had been able to take advantage of the uneven terrain in his designs, but the construction of certain features, particularly the terrace which had to be built from scratch, required hard work from the local labour-force. The family lived in the "big house," dubbed "the château" by the villagers, a long two-storey structure, covered with shingles in the style of country houses of the time. Sixteen bedrooms were scarcely enough for family and guests, and the main dining room was often set for more than twenty-five. The living room opened onto the verandas and occupied almost the entire ground floor of the house. A gallery at the second-floor level provided an excellent balcony for our theatricals. Here, too, we children used to huddle in the shadows, long after we were believed to be sound asleep, listening to the music or the conversation of the grown-ups. My parents and their friends often gathered around the huge fireplace, discussing the political and social problems of the day. The young people preferred the smaller Turkish salon for their important discussions or less serious chats.

When we first came to Saint-Irénée my father had bought two handsome St. Bernard dogs, which the local farmers often accused of attacking their sheep at night. True or false, my father always made good any claims. As it happened, we also possessed a black sheep, the devoted companion of our two dogs. It used to amuse us to see the inseparable trio trotting about happily without the two alleged villains ever doing the slightest harm to the weaker member. Perhaps, being a black sheep, he was more wicked than the two giants.

Like our parents, we children always had several guests of our own, and high spirits continually reigned. Maman loved to fill the house with lilac, peonies, and sweet peas and it was often my duty to look after the numerous bouquets, a pleasant task but tedious at times when other distractions beckoned. Music, games, and outings of all kinds followed one another. Ah, those picnics when we jolted along in a hay-wagon decked with willow boughs singing all the while! And the delightful trips aboard our yacht Margota–from the name of my eldest sister, Marguérite–to picturesque Île-aux-Coudres. There were also interminable tennis matches and swimming, either in the river or in the indoor pool, filled with icy sea-water on which the less brave could drift in a sort of little punt. And there were billiards and bowling and, for the inveterate bridge-players, the little Japanese salon in one of the pavilions.

Tom, our Chinese laundryman, lived over the wash-house, next door to the generator that furnished our electricity. One July evening there was a terrible thunderstorm and lightning struck very close to the generating plant, plunging us all into total darkness. When he made his usual tour of the grounds next day, my father stopped to ask Tom whether the thunder and lightning had frightened him. Tom replied with a broad smile: "Easy conscience never afraid."

On other levels were the vegetable garden, orchard, pigeon coop, hen-house, and stables. A reservoir fed by a mountain stream also supplied ice in winter for use during the following summer. Finally, there was a smaller house where our MacDonald cousins, of whom Papa was guardian, spent the summers and where we sometimes came when the weather was cold, since it was winterized. Close by was the greenhouse, so indispensable to the gardens and the flower-beds that edged the lawns and the rustic baskets filled with geraniums and nasturtiums. And since in this region everything grows very quickly during the short summers, a great many flowering shrubs perfumed the pathways, the longest of which was appropriately called the Lovers' Lane. On fine, calm evenings, when the moon turned the river to silver for as far as the eye could see and the starry sky was lit up by the northern lights whose faint rustling we sometimes fancied we could hear, this spot seemed to us a paradise on earth.

The daily arrival of the cruise ships of the Richelieu Company provided a welcome diversion for natives and vacationers alike. Young and old rushed to the dock to greet the travellers or chat with friends. One of the big white ships was skippered by Captain Joseph Simard of Baie-Saint-Paul, a handsome and courteous man whose sons founded the shipyard at Sorel. Our next stop was always that other meeting-place, the post office, to discuss the events of the day as we waited for the mail to be sorted.

Mr. Justice Joseph Lavergne and his wife, who was renowned for her great sense of humour, lived at Les Sablons; their son, Armand, a witty speaker and well-known Quebec nationalist, was very active in politics. Every summer the Hotel Charlevoix welcomed back a number of Montrealers whose children grew up with us. Among these were Sir Joseph and Lady Pope and two future lieutenant governors of Quebec: Narcisse Perodeau and Sir Evariste Leblanc. At *Hauterive*, the neighbouring property to ours, lived Sir Adolphe and Lady Routhier, old friends of my parents. Sir Adolphe, an Admiralty judge, was known for his writings, especially the words of our national anthem, *O Canada*. A brilliant conversationalist, he was always ready to provide occasional verse, such as the following when my brother took his first step:

C'est aujourd'hui le six septembre
De Jacques croissent les appâts;
La joie est grande dans la chambre
Il a fait ses premiers pas.
Mais il en fera bien d'autres
S'il suit son père exactement,
Pour s'unir aux bons apôtres
Qui composent le Parlement. . . .

or less gay at the end of a lovely summer:

Voici la saison qui s'achève
Elle a passé comme un beau rêve
C'est l'heure triste des adieux
Adieu Gil'Mont et Hauterive
Le flot m'emporte à la dérive
Loin de vos bords délicieux.

Le ciel est gris, le vent d'automne
Chante sa plainte monotone
Dans les grands arbres dépouillés . . .
Passez vite, hiver que j'abhorre
Et nous pourrons reprendre encore
Nos beaux rêves ensoleillés.

Lady Routhier, the daughter of Judge Mondelet and one of the leading hostesses in Quebec City, had maintained the custom of presenting light drawing room comedies; her husband and their daughter, Angeline, an exquisite and very cultivated woman whom we called *tante* Ange, excelled in these. Every August on Maman's birthday this adopted aunt organized a theatrical evening to which everyone holidaying in and around Saint-Irénée, as well as the local population, was invited. Even we children performed in brief plays or sketches, a pleasant way to spend part of our vacation. One summer when *tante* Ange was travelling, our English governess took a notion to replace her and had us present *The Merry Widow* with a Prince Danilo of eleven and a widow of the same age. The audience was somewhat astonished by this unusual program.

The Eucharistic Congress of 1910 made a deep impression upon me. At the request of Mgr. Bruchési, then Archbishop of Montreal and a friend of my father's, my parents entertained an Italian bishop at our house, which caused considerable commotion. During the congress, the Archbishop of Westminster, Mgr. Bourne, had expressed the opinion in an address in Notre-Dame church that "the English language should be the vehicle of the Faith . . . . We must in future ally the Catholic religion and the English language." Henri Bourassa rose and in an extemporary speech declared: "Catholicism should be neither English nor French but essentially Catholic. The Church should not lean now on one race, now on another, it should lean on all the races . . . . Providence has willed . . . that there should be in America a separate corner where social, religious, and political conditions most nearly approach those that the Church teaches us are the most desirable conditions for society . . . . Relations between the civil and religious authorities are excellent . . . . We are only a handful in number, but we still matter and we have the right to live . . . . "[8] Heated discussions followed at our house, for our guest, not being one of us, could not always grasp the fine points of our various national problems, such as the Manitoba school question, the bitterness between the Ontario Orangemen and the Quebec Catholics, and especially the fact that our province was far from passionately devoted to England.

Besides finance and politics, my father was interested in the young people in his riding and particularly in the education they received. To help raise standards he founded a school at Saint-Irénée and brought teaching nuns from France to staff it. This convent, which was maintained entirely at his expense, existed for some ten years and enrolled, in all, several hundred pupils, both boarders and day-pupils. Unfortunately the undertaking did not please everyone. The provincial authorities and the *curé* were especially angry and the latter, an out-and-out Liberal in politics, never quite forgave my father. Because of all these difficulties, the school had to close its doors and the nuns left Saint-Irénée. Among a number of young people who benefited from my father's generosity and later achieved success in life were the writer Jean-Charles Harvey, the author of the controversial novel *Les Demi-civilisés*, Lorenzo Gauthier, an important Verdun businessman, and two missionaries, Father Arthur Tremblay, a Jesuit who died in Japan, and Father Joseph Harvey, of the White Fathers of Africa. *Le Pays*, a newspaper of the time, wrote as follows:

> Instruction at the *Couvent Sainte-Marie* is absolutely free, not only for day-pupils but for boarders; that is to say, none of the children who attend classes have to pay a cent for teaching, for books or for board. In 1907, the first year, there were 30 day-pupils. In 1912, 26 boarders and 92 day-pupils. Each year the two pupils who win the first prizes are sent at Mr. Forget's expense to a classical college or a convent, as the case may be.
>
> Sir Rodolphe Forget pays the entire cost of the Sainte-Marie school. This amounts to more than $3000 a year.
>
> This convent is situated near the beach in a magnificent setting and in an exceptionally healthful spot. It is provided with baths, electric lights, and so on.[9]

My father's interest in good causes was continuous. During a fund-raising campaign launched by the Notre-Dame Hospital in Montreal, he wrote to Mr. Tancrède Bienvenu, the hospital treasurer, promising that if the campaign managed to raise one hundred and fifty thousand dollars, he would add a personal donation of one hundred thousand dollars. A contemporary newspaper wrote of him as follows: "He is the friend of the poor and the afflicted, the aged and the infirm. For their welfare and relief, he gives unsparingly. In Charlevoix as in Montreal, he has encouraged and supported innumerable good works. And he does all this modestly, without stir, as if it were the simplest thing in the world."[10]

At this period it was possible for a member of parliament to represent two ridings. The 1911 election gave my father those of Montmorency and Charlevoix and also elected Henri Bourassa, Paul-Émile Lamarche, Armand Lavergne, and other Quebec nationalists to the House of Commons. As Conservatives, they had spoken out against Laurier's plan for a Canadian navy, maintaining that if there were war such a project would primarily help England and would surely bring conscription to Canada. The future, unfortunately, was to show how right they were. During the campaign, I remember hearing this mocking verse sung to the tune of *Le Petit Navire*:

> Sur le grand mât d'une corvette,
> L'amiral *Niobé* chantait,
> Disant d'une voix inquiète,
> Ces mots que la brise emportait:
> J'ai peur que mon parti chavire
> Comme en *Drummond-Arthabaska*
> Filez, filez, ô mon navire
> Car Bourassa m'attend là-bas![11]

My father was opposed in Charlevoix on that occasion by Lucien Cannon, a brilliant young lawyer who was elected to the House of Commons in 1917 and who later became a minister in the Mackenzie King cabinet. He sat in the legislative assembly of Quebec for some years and during the 1915-16 session actually introduced a bill to admit women to the Quebec Bar. Although the bill was not adopted, it showed a liberal spirit in its sponsor that was, to say the least, audacious at that time.

Recalling that particular campaign later, Lucien Cannon told me of a speech he had made in Baie-Saint-Paul, a Conservative stronghold. Not wishing to antagonize his audience, he spoke of my father in very flattering terms before proceeding to discuss the Liberal platform. He was disconcerted when the old man who was driving him to the dock after the meeting remarked, "Ah, Mr. Cannon, when our Mr. Forget can't come himself, he always sends very good men to replace him." However, he consoled himself with the thought that calm had been maintained till the end of the meeting, which was something at least at a time and in a region where election customs were far from mild. Towards 1880, the story goes, after an election campaign that had been marked by a great many free-for-alls, the supporters of the defeated candidate in Charlevoix tore down a bridge in their rage, and there were even dead and wounded among their opponents.

Echoes of the 1911 campaign reached my convent, which was normal enough since most of the pupils' parents were involved. Corinne Dupuis and I mingled devotion and politics on polling day by lighting blue vigil lights–the colour of the Conservatives–beside the altar of the Virgin, while the Lemieux and Belcourt girls lit red ones–the colour of the Liberals–beside the altar of the Sacred Heart. That evening our joy and the sorrow of our Liberal companions were equally great when the Conservative victory was announced. I was especially proud that Papa was now going to be the member for two ridings. On his return to Montreal after the election, he was welcomed in triumph by hundreds of friends and supporters who had gathered at Viger Station to meet him, and I was permitted to leave school that day to take part in the great celebration. Because of the way we were brought up then, there was no question of our taking a direct part in what our parents did. However, they always found a way to let us witness the important events of their lives.

III

Gilded Youth

During their travels in Europe my parents had appreciated the beauty of Paris and they wished to have a residence built for themselves in Montreal that would reflect French styles. Here is another evidence of my father's nationalist feelings, for he wanted to have a house that would be quite different from the costly mansions in the western part of the city, most of them English in design. Thus he bought a lot on the upper part of Ontario Avenue near Pine Avenue, and engaged the architects Marchand and Haskell; Mr. Marchand had studied for many years in Paris, which made him eminently fitted for the task. Though construction was begun in 1912, the house was not completed till after the war because furniture and materials that had been ordered from Europe could not be delivered. The piano, a Steinway on which the American artist Blackwell had painted views of *Gil'Mont* and miniatures of the children, occupied a corner of the drawing-room and a prominent place in our lives, for we all loved music. Most of our servants lived with us, among them Marc Gauthier of Saint-Irénée and his wife, who were in our service for forty years. Marc, at first our coachman and in charge of the ponies, now saw to the maintenance of the property. I was godmother to his son, André, who is today an able businessman of imposing height and weight. Years later, when I stood for election in Verdun, he very kindly allowed me to stop and rest in his home whenever I liked.

As soon as vacation time came round, we returned to Saint-Irénée, where friends soon came to join us. Among visitors to *Gil'Mont* I recall Lord Grey, whose obvious interest in all aspects of Canadian life we all remembered with pleasure; Mr. Justice Charles Archer, his wife, and their daughter Pauline, who became

Mrs. Georges Vanier, all lifelong friends; and the well-known poet, Louis Frechette, a distant relative of Maman's for whom, with his usual ease, he wrote a sonnet in our album, evoking a supposed legend about our house:

> Cette villa qui brille au soleil et dessine,
> Sur le fond vert des bois, ses paradis rêvés,
> Cette villa qui tient les regards captivés,
> Vous fait bien des jaloux, ma charmante cousine.
>
> On dit qu'un jour, au fond de la forêt voisine
> Pour orner ce palais féérique, vous avez,
> Précieux talisman par vos soins retrouvés,
> Acheté les secrets de quelque mélusine.
>
> On prétend à l'appui, qu'autour du gai manoir,
> Une baguette en main, sitôt que vient le soir,
> Une femme paraît, de longs voiles coiffée.
>
> Mais moi qui vous connais, je sais même de loin
> Que pour charmer ainsi, vous n'avez eu besoin
> Du secours de personne, et que c'est vous la fée.

Other guests were the Honourable Arthur Meighen, then solicitor general in the Borden government, a brilliant young man who, Papa predicted, would some day be Prime Minister of Canada, and René du Roure, a McGill professor well known in Montreal intellectual circles and a great friend of Stephen Leacock.

In 1913 the 65th Regiment came for the second time to hold its annual manoeuvres in Charlevoix, setting up camp at *Gil'Mont* on the invitation of my father, its honorary Lieutenant-Colonel. Sir Sam Hughes, the Minister of Militia, Sir Ian Hamilton, and Major Édouard Panet came to inspect the reservists, and among the members of their staff was a charming young officer in the Grenadier Guards, John Bassett by name. He later became director of the Montreal *Gazette*, and his son owned the well-known Toronto *Telegram*. On this occasion John gave me the scarlet plume from his shako, a gift I received with great pride, not knowing that it would earn the young man a severe reprimand from his superiors, who did not much favour this kind of generosity.

Our grounds were covered with white tents, and you can imagine the bustle and excitement as the troops simulated a battle, man-oeuvring over hills and valleys, exciting the children, and arousing the curiosity of their elders. How improbable a real war seemed to us then. An open-air Mass celebrated under the June sun, in an imposing setting between the height of land and the river, was particularly impressive. The regiment had a remarkable choir and, at the moment of the elevation of the Host, a royal salute was fired from the summit of our hill. The customary banquet was a joyful affair and, besides the usual speeches, there were humorous songs composed for the occasion. The regimental chap-lain, Captain Deschamps, who later became Coadjutor Archbishop of Montreal, often returned to Saint-Irénée for a few weeks' vaca-tion in later years.

We thus had the occasion to entertain priests who were also friends. For instance, there was Mgr. Paul Bruchesi who had inher-ited a great love for music from his Italian forebears and was always willing to sing Botrel's songs to the children (his nephew Jean, my father's godson, is a well-known writer and diplomat). We had good-natured and interminable arguments with Mgr. Cyrille Labrecque of Quebec, and Father Émile Chaussende, a young French missionary, was our partner in delightful tennis matches. Father Louis Trudeau, a Dominican, came accompanied on one occasion by Father Georges Ceslas Rutten, O.P., a Belgian senator and sociologist then visiting Montreal. The latter wrote in our album: "May I not have been the guest of a day who goes on his way and never again returns. Short stays sometimes make long memories." This day-to-day association with wise and cul-tivated men was as pleasant as it was valuable.

On the 20th of September, 1913, the second anniversary of the victory of the Borden government, the electors of Montmorency and Charlevoix gave a big banquet in my father's honour at Sainte-Anne-de-Beaupré. A parade of twenty-five cars full of ministers and members of parliament, my father in the lead, drove from Quebec City to Sainte-Anne. All our family was present. The guests of honour, the mayors, and notables of the parishes, some five hundred in all, took their places in the banquet hall and in the corridor of the hotel. But as about two thousand people had come to cheer the hero of the day, including several hundred from outside Quebec, most had to wait outside until the meal was over. For their benefit the festivities which were to be carried out inside were repeated in the open air. Congratulatory telegrams from Prime Minister Borden and many others were read to the crowd. In his speech after the banquet, my father said that, despite the wishes of some of his opponents, no law had yet been found that would prevent him from representing two ridings and he would continue his efforts to make Quebec City, the gateway to Canada, a great national port, and an industrial centre.

The respect and prestige that he commanded doubtless greatly contributed to the Conservatives' winning twenty-seven Quebec seats in the 1911 election, and one can only wonder why he was never a member of the Borden cabinet. He saw far into the future and his breadth of vision doubtless frightened many people whose own ideas were not so advanced. As well, he was the object of much jealousy. One version of the story goes that Borden offered him a ministry without portfolio but, as the English Protestants of Quebec would then have had no representative, my father declined in favour of Sir George Perley, the member for Argenteuil. "I shall never forget this generous action," Borden is supposed to have said, and shortly afterwards my father was made a knight of the Order of St. Michael and St. George of the British Empire. Another version has it that Armand Lavergne, who was then succeeding Bourassa as leader of the Quebec nationalists, did not wish to see my father enter the cabinet where, as a broker, he would be able to profit from government projects. I believe that my father would never have agreed to sacrifice his progressive ideas to the narrower ones of the Quebec of those days. In addition, his outspokenness–an unusual trait among politicians–irritated many of them.

After I had graduated from the Convent of the Sacred Heart, I stayed at home, leading the life of a typical young girl of the times–shopping, going to parties and, now and then, to a play carefully selected by my parents. It was customary for girls to study literature, music, singing, and Italian, so that they would be accomplished and cultivated wives. The domestic arts were not neglected, however, for it was very important that a woman should know how to manage a household and prepare meals. I was, therefore, sent to the kitchen to profit from the advice of our cook, a *cordon bleu* named Freda. She did not in the least appreciate my intrusion into her domain and said, "Mademoiselle, I have quite enough to do as it is, just let me work in peace." Clearly I would not obtain my cookery badge here. For a whole year I studied Italian with Professor Giuseppe Nelli, a native of Florence, and, to my great joy, I was able after a few months to speak the language reasonably well. One summer day I accompanied my father when he inspected the workmen employed in the building of the Quebec-Saguenay Railway. They were almost all Europeans, including many Italians, and Papa turned to me and said, "Now's your chance to try out your Italian." Enunciating very clearly, I spoke a few friendly words to them but, to my regret, they seemed not to understand. Seeing my distress, one of them said simply, "Me no Italian, me Pole." When Italy entered World War II, I learned that Professor Nelli had been interned along with a number of other Italians. Surely this elderly man, who had lived in Canada for more than forty years, would not have harmed anyone. The authorities soon realized this too and he was released.

The oyster-supper held every November to raise money for the Deaf and Dumb Institute was an important social event in which all Montreal took part. The year's debutantes waited on the guests and sold roses for ten cents, carnations for five cents, and bottles of good wine for only seventy-five cents. How happy I felt as I went for the first time to this party of which I had heard so much. Here I renewed my acquaintance with Pierre Casgrain, a young lawyer much praised for his seriousness and charm, whom I had already met at a tea-dance when I was fifteen. "I'd like," my partner had said, "to introduce you to one of my friends whom my parents very much admire. Though he's an orphan of independent means, he prefers grubbing away at his law studies to an easy life of travel and adventure." Remembering his teasing but indifferent remarks to the little school-girl of those days, I didn't feel that I had particularly attracted his attention this time either. So what was my joyful surprise to receive from him the next day my first bouquet of roses. When he then invited me to the theatre, my father insisted that we should be at least four in the party. So Pierre asked a comrade and one of my friends to go with us.

The role of chaperone sometimes fell to my brother, Gilles, and it was he who accompanied us to the Saint-Regis, a famous restaurant where I had long dreamed of going. Shyly I had already refused several things when a kick under the table from Gilles compelled me to accept some cherry ice cream. "If you'd turned that down," he informed me afterwards, "I would never have gone out with you again." All this to show that *tête-à-têtes* between young people were scarcely encouraged in those days. Nor were they permitted to be alone in the family drawing room. One evening Pierre, now my fiancé, dared to kiss me behind Papa, who was reading his newspaper; the latter informed my mother later that he had witnessed the whole scene in his glasses. Times have changed since then!

When Pierre asked for my hand, Papa thought it well to point out that a difference in age of ten years might present certain problems. My future husband replied that this did not worry him in the least. He had had very little family life and was looking forward to having a home of his own. He had lost his mother when he was three and his father when he was twenty and still lived with his grandmother. She had known the sorrow of seeing her seven children die as well as all her grand-children except Pierre, who looked after her till her death at eighty-eight. When I reprimanded the children, he would often say to me: "Don't scold them too much, it must be so nice to be spoiled by a mother. I never knew that joy."

On my wedding-day, the 19th of January, 1916, the weather was splendid. It had snowed heavily the day before and now the trees sparkled in the sun; I felt that all this beauty was a special gift from heaven and a sign of happiness for me. When I reached the church, I was shocked to learn that my fiancé was not yet there. The guests were already in their places and I had to wait for a quarter of an hour, which to me seemed a century, before I could make my entrance on my father's arm. After the ceremony I learned that the Ottawa train bringing the best man, Pierre's cousin, the Honourable Tom Chase Casgrain, then postmaster general in the Borden cabinet, had been delayed by the previous day's storm.

During the reception that followed at our house, I was urged to sing and had the more or less happy notion of bidding farewell to my family with a touching ballad of the period, *La vieille maison grise*. A touch of comedy immediately lightened the atmosphere when one of the guests, moved by too much champagne, had to be forcibly prevented from accompanying us on our honeymoon. We departed for New York that evening and a few days later set sail for Cuba where I discovered, while visiting pineapple and orange plantations, the taste of fruit that has ripened in the sun. It was also on this island that I was first struck by the sight of wretched poverty and extreme wealth existing side by side. Events of recent years could be anticipated even then and scarcely surprised me when they did occur. We were still in Cuba when news came of the fire in the parliament buildings in Ottawa. The first reports announced the death of two members of parliament and, as my father then sat in the House of Commons, I knew several anxious hours. Fortunately Pierre was able to get in touch with him and set my mind at ease.

IV

End of a Dream

Our first home in Montreal was on Bishop Street, then a calm and peaceful spot far from the business section of town. Like every other bride, I was delighted to be in a place of my own. In March 1916, my parents gave a benefit on Ontario Avenue for the newly formed 150th Battalion, which was commanded by Colonel Barré. The drawing rooms were filled with guests and I can still see the women in their magnificent gowns on the arms of officers in dress uniforms, swirling to the strains of melodic waltzes played by the orchestra. The chandeliers glittered and masses of flowers gave a fairy-tale brilliance to the scene. Anyone watching the dancers circle so joyfully could guess that they were all trying to forget for an evening the tragic times in which we were then living. These soldiers were soon to leave Canada, and several of them would never return. This was my first ball but my pleasure quickly gave way to sadness when I thought of how uncertain the future was. The years that followed confirmed these feelings and were to deeply mark my attitude towards life.

My father and Pierre often talked about the problems of French Canada, especially its poverty and its lack of industrial development. Like Henri Bourassa, my father believed in the future of Quebec and of Canada. He appreciated the justice of certain English laws that had been adopted by our country, but at the same time, he encouraged French businessmen to invest here, especially in Quebec, as the English had been doing for many years.

When war was declared in 1914, he paraded with his regiment, the 65th, through the streets of Montreal, proud to see in his compatriots the generosity and gallantry they had inherited from their ancestors–an emotion I myself felt in 1939. As the war continued, Prime Minister Sir Robert Borden gradually became convinced that the only way to obtain enough recruits for the Canadian forces was to impose compulsory military service, a measure Bourassa and the other nationalists had already opposed during the Boer War at the turn of the century. A popular movement against conscription for the defence of the British Empire was accompanied by rioting in Quebec City and Montreal. The politicians who favoured the measure formed a coalition government under the leadership of Prime Minister Borden, who then appealed to the people. Laurier, abandoned by many of his former colleagues, and the other Quebec Liberals spoke out against conscription. My father also opposed conscription and now decided to retire from politics.

At this point, my husband made up his mind to seek the Liberal candidacy in Charlevoix, where Charles Angers of La Malbaie had already entered the race. One or other of them had to obtain the endorsement of Sir Wilfrid Laurier. Young, and dynamic and already a well-known Montreal lawyer, Pierre won the leader's approval and thus became the official Liberal candidate in the election of December 1917. I accompanied him during the campaign, undertaking journeys that, in view of the season, sometimes became veritable odysseys. Indeed, the snow and the cold were of little help to the candidates. Crossing the St. Lawrence in winter could be alarming, for the strongly-built oarsmen sometimes had to drag their loaded boats across moving ice and thrust them back into the fast-flowing water. Once, when we were crossing from Baie-Saint-Paul to Île-aux-Coudres, for my own safety I had to be tied to the bottom of the boat.

At that time, as there were few newspapers and no radio or television, the only entertainment of the villagers was visiting one another and exchanging their views and ideas. The people who lived on Île-aux-Coudres grew potatoes and caught dolphins. Though very friendly and intelligent, most of them had very little education. Sometimes even the mayor could barely sign his name. (Teachers then earned between seventy-five and one hundred and fifty dollars a year.) The influence of the *curé* was very great, and often no decision would be made without consulting him. There were two churches on the island and every Sunday after High

Mass the parishioners gathered outside to listen to what was called *la criée*, a sort of spoken newspaper informing the population of the business and events of the week to come. It was on this island that Jacques Cartier landed on the 7th of September, 1535, with the hundred and ten men of his crew and their two chaplains to celebrate Mass and plant a cross beside the sea. He chose the name Île-aux-Coudres because of the abundance of hazel trees (in French, *coudrier*). It has now become a tourist centre and attracts a great many artists, including the painter Jean-Paul Lemieux, who spends several months there every year.

My husband's manager at Les Éboulements was J.H. Tremblay, the mayor of the village, known familiarly as J.H. to distinguish him from all the other Tremblays. I recently visited this old man of ninety-one, whom I had not seen for many years, and our meeting was very pleasant for us both. No one would suspect his age, seeing him so erect and full of life. He told me of his sorrow at the news of Pierre's sudden death. "Every time he came to see me," he said, "I welcomed him like the son of the house because I was very fond of him and knew how sincere and honest he was." Gradually, as we talked, he began to speak of his youth. In 1898 he won the Prince of Wales prize at the Normal School in Quebec. The competition involved writing an essay on a subject that had been developed by one of the teachers in a speech. J.H., who had a prodigious memory, had transcribed the speech almost word for word so that the teacher had asked whether J.H. had by any chance seen the text. Armed with his prize, the new graduate set out for the North Shore and the village of La Tabatière, where he was to teach. There were twenty-five pupils in his class and I was astonished to learn that there were no Indians among them. "They were all English youngsters from Newfoundland," he told me. "So of course I had to speak English, which was easy because I was perfectly bilingual. To please them I even decorated a beautiful spruce tree at Christmas, but it was destroyed by fire during Midnight Mass, a great sorrow for both me and my pupils. During the winter Father Gaudreault, the *curé*, had to go to Quebec and heavy snowstorms prevented him from returning. One evening while I was correcting exercises, I heard a knock and found a young Indian couple carrying a tiny coffin. Their baby had just died and they wanted to see him rest in holy ground. I advised them to spend the night in the nearby hotel and go to the cemetery next morning and dig the grave themselves. To my surprise they returned the following day to tell me that everything was ready and that they would like me to say some prayers before the burial. Because the *curé* was away, they had come to me, the teacher. Plucking up my courage, I put on the priest's chasuble, took the aspergillum and a bottle I believed held holy water, and went with the parents to the cemetery. I read the appropriate prayers from the missal and sprinkled the mortal remains of the baby. The young Indians then departed, slightly consoled, and I went back to my work, conscious of having done a good deed. Eventually the snow melted and the *curé* returned. When he learned that I had officiated at a burial in his absence, he told me he would go and bless the grave and asked me to accompany him. It seemed to us that the water in the bottle I'd used was a bit cloudy. In fact, to our great surprise, it was maple sap. My blunder amused us both very much, but no one else ever knew of it."

After his return to Les Éboulements in 1907, J.H. married and bought the house where he still lives, which was formerly the Courthouse and Town Hall. He had the misfortune to lose his wife after fifty-two years of marriage, as well as his adopted daughter – he had no children of his own – and his wife's sister now keeps house for him. "You see, Madame," he went on, "I am like a cypress which has watched almost all the people of the parish grow up. Unfortunately the world grows emptier and emptier around me and if I lose my sister-in-law I'd have to go into an old-age home." As we parted, I saw how moved he was recalling these memories, realizing that this meeting might be our last.

The day after the 1917 election, in which my husband was victorious – despite the defeat of the Liberals under Laurier – we set out from Baie-Saint-Paul by sleigh to go home for Christmas and to collect our baby, whom we had left in my mother's care. We had to pass through the woods and over the capes of Charlevoix in a carriole drawn by two horses in tandem. The road, which was too narrow to allow two vehicles to pass, was banked high with snow for, in the words of Léonce Boivin, "when it snows in the capes, it snows by sacks-full." On one occasion we had to pass the sleighs of some farmers who were on their way to Quebec City to sell their Christmas turkeys; to avoid sinking into the snow, our driver had to spread our thick buffalo robes—so essential to travellers in our rigorous climate—for the horses to walk on. The short relay-stop at La Barrière was very welcome, giving us a chance to warm up and recover our strength before resuming our journey to Quebec City, where we arrived at eleven o'clock in the evening, having covered eighty miles in fourteen hours. It was during this election that the right to vote in federal elections was granted to a limited number of Canadian women, the mothers, wives, and sisters of members of the armed services.

In the new year I accompanied Pierre to Ottawa for the opening of Parliament. Since most of the parliament buildings had recently been destroyed by fire, the members sat in the museum and it was here, from the gallery, that I witnessed stormy sittings when the old leader, Sir Wilfrid Laurier, had to face former comrades-in-arms who had broken with him over the conscription question. Sir Wilfrid and Lady Laurier invited Pierre and me to dinner, the first of several such occasions, and I often joined in evening bridge parties while the men were in Parliament. Lady Laurier was a charming woman with a gift for putting her guests very much at ease.

In January of the following year, my father went to Baie-Saint-Paul to observe the progress of the railway that he so much wished to see completed. There he fell gravely ill and my mother had to rush him back to Montreal. He was immediately confined to bed and was never to leave it. Eleven days before his death, ill as he was, he called together the directors of the Quebec Railway to complete the arrangements for the sale of the Quebec-Saguenay Railway to the government. His talents and mind were still untouched and he discussed the final clauses and wound up the contract with perfect clarity. A few days afterwards his friend, Mgr. Bruchési, came to administer the last sacraments. Mgr. Bruchési himself was soon stricken by an illness that forced him to retire from public life till his death some twenty years later. My father died at fifty-seven—just two days after Sir Wilfrid Laurier. As a number of members of parliament and other important people wished to attend my father's funeral, the service had to be delayed for two days to enable them to pay homage to both these great Canadians.

Six months later, in July 1919, the first train between La Malbaie and Saint-Joachim was put into service. We watched it pass with aching hearts, thinking that the one who had fought for twenty-five years towards this end was not there to see the final achievement. Mgr. Léonce Boivin spoke of my father in these terms:

> We owe the railway line that links La Malbaie and Saint-Joachim to him and only to him. Great will-power was needed to undertake such a project and carry it through. Mountains had to be sliced or pierced, and the coves and Laurentian headlands skirted. At the same time he had to ensure that there would be sufficient business to support the line. Thus, he built a factory at Chute-Nairn, knowing that abundant electric power was nearby, as well as mountains covered with timber, iron, and everything else that would be required. He was a powerful man who might have transformed the whole region if he had lived. He did good all through his life, helping the poor and giving generously to charitable institutions and other worthy causes. His memory is still green and fresh. "[1]

In 1923, to honour my father's memory, the people of the county decided to erect a bronze bust, the work of our artist, Henri Hébert. An argument arose between La Malbaie and Baie-Saint-Paul over where the monument should be located and, to settle the difficulty, our family was asked to deed over a plot of land at the bottom of our property. So the memorial stands at *Gil'Mont* in Saint-Irénée, close to the road. The Little Sisters of St. Francis bought our property in 1946 and operated it first as a school of domestic science and later as a home for handicapped people. In the autumn of 1965 a fire destroyed the big house; it has never been rebuilt.

For several years our families returned each summer to *Gil'Mont*, as my father had wished. He had even made provision for the expenses of these vacations in his will. A new generation now played hide-and-seek and built castles in the sand. Improved roads put Saint-Irénée a mere fifteen minutes' drive from La Malbaie and holidayers from our two beaches met at the golf course, the swimming pool or the ballroom of the Manoir Richelieu. In 1919 the Honourable William Lyon Mackenzie King came to visit us and, at his residence, Kingsmere, I later saw terraces with white balustrades that he told me had been inspired by those he had seen at *Gil'Mont*. In 1942, at the request of the federal government, the property was put at the disposal of the Duke of Kent, then visiting Canada, for a few days' relaxation. The servants were much impressed to see the Duke and his party taking morning dips in the icy waters of the pool. They also noticed his Highness's obvious fondness for such simple Canadian dishes as *cretons* and blueberry pie; he preferred these to all the elaborate and dainty courses served to him. We had withdrawn to the cottage, our winter house, and one day the temporary host of *Gil'Mont* invited us to tea. During our conversation he told us of his admiration for this charming corner of Quebec, which had completely won his heart.

Between election campaigns my husband used to take advantage of the summer months to visit distant parts of his riding which, after changes in the electoral map, extended to Blanc Sablon, not far from the shores of Newfoundland. On one such journey, he found himself on the same boat as the apostolic delegate who was visiting the fishermen of the coast. Mgr. A. Cassulo was over six feet tall and weighed about 275 pounds. One morning during heavy fog the boat ran onto a rock near the Magdalen Islands. There was no panic and the captain asked the passengers not to try to leave the ship until he gave the order. As the tide rose, the ship began to take in water and threatened to capsize. The fog lifted, revealing a fleet of fishing boats that had come to help in taking off the passengers. One by one each of them climbed down a narrow emergency ladder, but in Mgr. Cassulo's case the matter was more complicated. His great size barred him from any such feat and it was decided finally to use a block and tackle to lower him into one of the boats. He was wrapped in a heavy fishing-net and eased down the hull of the ship. Suddenly the net caught and one of the fishermen shouted loudly, "Holy Virgin! Watch out, you'll dump the Pope!" much to the hilarity of all. Once on land, everyone proceeded to the village, where the people did everything possible to welcome their unexpected guests. The next morning, a Sunday, Mgr. Cassulo celebrated Mass and delivered a short sermon. Unaware of how easily our people make use of sacred terms usually reserved for the Church, he said, in his musical voice and with the Italian accent that gave an amusing note to all his words, that he commended the faith of the Magdalen Islanders who in their hours of trial "knew how to pray."

In his second campaign, in 1921, Pierre's opponent was the Honourable Mr. Belley, postmaster general in the Meighen government. This was a very closely contested election, for my husband, still a very young man, had to face an experienced politician. Just before nominations, which were to be followed by a big rally, Pierre became seriously ill with pleurisy at Baie-Saint-Paul. There could be no question of moving him to the hospital so the doctors confined him to his small hotel room. I therefore telephoned Quebec City and asked them to send a replacement. Ernest Lapointe, then also a member of the Commons and a man who respected everyone and was highly respected in return, came to lend his support. On the day of the meeting, almost a thousand people were crowded into the grounds of the hotel, including a number who had crossed the river from Île-aux-Coudres to listen to the speakers. At the sight of all these people, Mr. Lapointe decided on a touch of theatre and persuaded me to offer my husband's excuses myself. This was the first occasion, moreover, when women were entitled to use the right to vote that Borden had given them in 1918. Mr. Lapointe informed the crowd that someone close at hand would explain why the candidate was not present, and to their surprise, I delivered my first political speech. My love for Pierre gave me the courage for an action that was considered very daring at that time. Since there was a rumour going about in the riding that my husband was hiding because he was afraid of his opponent, I said, "It's true that my husband is ill and he has sent what is dearest to him in all the world next to his constituency–his wife–to offer his apologies. He is counting on your support in this election." The effect Mr. Lapointe had wished for occurred, and my husband was re-elected.

As soon as I returned to Montreal, Lady Drummond, Mrs. Henri Gérin-Lajoie, and others who were interested in women's rights and had heard of the part I had played in my husband's election campaign, came to see me. And so I began my struggle for women's rights–a struggle that in Canada is far from over.

V

Battles Thrice Six I Have Seen

At that time in traditionalist Quebec our political leaders refused to admit the importance of women's suffrage. The party in power and the opposition alike always agreed, on some pretext or other, to deny women the right to vote. They professed not to realize that the provincial governments hold almost exclusive jurisdiction over laws dealing with social welfare, education, and labour–in short, everything that touches the family most closely. This attitude was all the more shocking as women had exercised the right to vote more than a century earlier. In fact, Quebec was then the only part of the British Empire where such a state of affairs existed. The Constitutional Act of 1791 established a legislative assembly in Lower Canada and granted the right to vote to all persons possessing certain property qualifications. Considering themselves to be persons, the women voted. In *Les Deux Papineau*, Senator David describes a scene during the stormy election of 1809 when several Montreal women, including Mrs. Papineau, voted for Joseph Papineau. The voice-vote was customary at that time and Mrs. Papineau announced for all to hear: "I vote for my son, Joseph Papineau, because I believe he is a good and faithful subject."[1] Unfortunately a law was passed by the parliament of United Canada in 1843 depriving women of the right to vote, and it remained in effect for years to come. The women of Quebec were thus denied a right that they alone in the British Empire had enjoyed for half a century. This legislation was very retrograde, especially when one considers how much these women had contributed to the building of our country from the earliest days of settlement. It is clear that some men feared that their authority would be weakened if women were allowed to take an active part in public affairs.

Before World War I, when the efforts of the English suffragettes were capturing the attention of the Canadian population, Mrs. Emmeline Pankhurst, one of their number, came to Canada in 1911 for a series of speaking engagements. She made a profound impression upon the public but I remember hearing some quite unflattering comments about her and her companions.

In 1913, the Montreal Suffrage Association was founded. This organization, whose purpose is clearly indicated by its title, was closely connected with the Women's Christian Temperance Union, headed by Mrs. John Scott, which advocated total prohibition and believed that the fight against alcoholism would have more success if women had the suffrage. They gradually broadened their activities and sought to have the municipal code amended to permit women to sit on school boards and give married women who were property owners the right to vote in municipal elections. The granting of the federal vote to some women in 1917 opened a breach in the dike and in 1918 this right was extended to all women by the Women's Suffrage Act. Quebec lagged behind by refusing women this right in provincial elections.

In 1919, after serious study, the members of the Montreal Suffrage Association came to the conclusion that in a province with a French-speaking majority, women's suffrage could only be obtained with the co-operation of French-speaking Canadians. It must be admitted, however, that very few people in our society were in favour of such a liberal measure.

Hoping that the two ethnic groups would soon be more closely linked, the M.S.A. decided to disband on the 22nd of May, 1919. From that date until 1922 no organization was officially concerned with the struggle for the vote for women except a special committee of the Montreal Women's Club, which kept the spark alive by putting the question on the agenda of all their meetings.

Among those concerned with this question was Dr. Grace Ritchie-England, an extremely intelligent woman, the first of her sex to practise medicine in Quebec. She once told me that she had been chosen to give the valedictory address at her graduation from McGill in 1888. In the draft of her speech she expressed the hope that the university would admit women to the faculty of medicine. She had to submit her text to the principal, Sir William Dawson, who was scandalized by that particular passage and struck it out. At the official ceremony, however, she decided to reinsert it. Sir William's reactions are not known but Lord Lansdowne, the Governor General of the time who was the guest of honour, commented favourably upon her words. This incident clearly indicates the differences of opinions that shook our society in those days. When Dr. England came to request my cooperation in her work, she chanced to meet Maman, who said, "So you're the one who's been indoctrinating my ugly duckling," and Dr. England replied, "On the contrary, your daughter is a beautiful swan."

In 1921 some English-speaking and French-speaking women came together to decide how best to form a bilingual association. Present at this meeting were Mrs. Henri Gérin-Lajoie, the president of the *Fédération nationale Saint-Jean-Baptiste*, Professor Carrie Derick, Lady Drummond, Dr. Grace Ritchie-England, Mrs. Walter Lyman, Miss Idola Saint-Jean, Mrs. John Scott, and myself. The *Comité provincial pour le Suffrage féminin* (The Provincial Suffrage Committee) was founded with Mrs. Henri Gérin-Lajoie and Mrs. Walter Lyman as joint presidents. It was stipulated that the committee would be apolitical and would devote its efforts "to an educational campaign to persuade the public and the legislature that women do not wish to have the vote in order to change their sphere in life but rather to raise and improve the level of society in general."[2]

On the 9th of February, 1922, a delegation of about four hundred went to Quebec to ask the provincial government to grant the vote to women. Mrs. Gérin-Lajoie had taken me under her wing and, when she saw me literally trembling with fear as the time came for me to speak, she threw her astrakhan coat in a maternal gesture over my shoulders, which almost crushed me with its weight while providing a comforting warmth. I dared to say to Prime Minister Taschereau, who had received us in the dining room in the Legislature, that the place he had chosen was quite in harmony with the viewpoint of our hosts since it was next to the kitchen, the place to which the ladies are generally relegated. Mr. Henry Miles, a member of the legislative council, pleaded our cause. As he was about to sit down, some members of the opposite camp pulled back his chair, causing him a nasty fall. Our

51

illusions and our hopes fell with him. After listening to us politely, Mr. Taschereau declared in private conversation that very day: "If the women of Quebec ever get the right to vote, they will not have got it from me."

The clergy, generally speaking, were opposed to votes for women, which was far from aiding our cause. However, the following letter from M. L'abbé L. Perrin, the *curé* of Notre-Dame, was published in *La Semaine réligieuse* on the 9th of December, 1921, and shows that all did not share the narrow views of the majority.

On the question of women's suffrage, there are three things to distinguish with care: 1. A question of principle; 2. A question of fact; 3. A question of appropriate timing.

1. *Question of principle.* As regards the first, I believe it should be expressed thus: Have women the right to vote? This question is open to debate. I have taught, because I believe it to be the truth, that under the present democratic system, which is based on popular suffrage, woman like man has the right to vote; that, married or not married, she supports the charges of the state and so has great and manifold interests in defending it; that to deprive her of the right to vote is to remove her most powerful means of defence; that a woman is a person and as such is inviolate in all that concerns political thought as well as in matters of morals or religion; and that, when she is excluded from the electorate, it cannot be said, according to the democratic axiom, that the law she has not made is the expression of the general will or that the government to which she does not consent is the legitimate representation of the governed.

During the middle ages women participated in elections in the commons and even in the estates-general, under the benevolent eye of the Church, and the acts in which they intervened were wise and universally recognized to be so; they voted and were still able to carry out their duties. The revival of Roman law during the Renaissance, followed by the Reformation and the repeated teachings of Luther, curtailed the electoral rights of women; the savagery and harshness of revolutionary customs abolished women's remaining rights in public life. In modern times the feminist movement revived and in all the civilized countries of the world, except France and Switzerland, the electoral rights of women have been restored.

Has the participation of women in public life brought those domestic upheavals that are so greatly feared? On the evidence of numerous commentators who have attentively followed social movements in Europe and Asia, the answer is in the negative–neither in the past nor at present.

That is what I have maintained on the question of principle, supported by weighty ecclesiastical and lay authorities. Others are free to maintain the opposite thesis. The question is open.

2. *Question of fact*. I have also said publicly that women's suffrage is a benefit to society and it is this point in particular that has been viewed with disfavour by a great many people. However, to deny it would be to show oneself singularly unfamiliar with contemporary social history. Even a superficial glance at social legislation in those countries where women have the right to vote will clearly indicate that many measures of great value to society have resulted. Here, in particular, evidence abounds, which no observer could presume to disregard.

Cardinal Vaughan of England agreed emphatically to women becoming involved in public affairs. Mgr. Ireland stated in a public address: "No one should despair of the world if women obtain the right to suffrage." The reigning Holy Father declared "that he wished to see women electors everywhere."

These words imply, of course that the female vote is not a social evil. Those who oppose granting the suffrage to women should not take their stand on the question of social benefit but rather on the principles of natural law; here everyone is free to draw his own conclusions and debate could continue indefinitely.

3. *Question of appropriate timing*. Finally, there is the third question, that of timing and this I have not yet mentioned, either directly or indirectly. Is it advisable at the present moment for Canadian women of the Catholic faith to concern themselves with political questions? The only authority competent to answer this question is that of our bishops, whose duty it is to direct us and to whose authority it is sweet and easy for us to submit, knowing the heavy burden they are required at times to bear and the anguish that often fills their hearts.

Believe me, yours very sincerely,
L. Perrin, p.s.s.

Inasmuch as this letter was written at a period when complete submission to the established authority was *de rigueur*–whether among the clergy or in governments or in society in general–it is difficult for us to pass judgment on the last part of M. L'abbé's letter on the question of timing. I believe that the demonstrations and confrontations we are experiencing today are linked to this obligatory submission in previous decades.

A few months later, on April 13, 1922, another letter from a high ecclesiastical authority appeared – this time in the daily *Le Canada* and taking an open position against female suffrage.

> *Collège Canadien*, Rome,
> March 19, 1922

His Grace Mgr. P. E. Roy
Archbishop of Séleucie, Quebec.

Your Grace,

I read with great interest your excellent and timely letter of the 17th of February last to the publicity committee of the Ladies of the diocese opposing female political suffrage and I endorse your letter with all my heart.

The entry of women into politics, even by merely voting, would be a misfortune for our province. Nothing justifies it, neither the natural law nor the good of society. The Roman authorities endorse our views, which are those of our entire episcopacy.

Our teachers in their instruction should take account of this directive.

Yours in Christ,

> L. N. Cardinal Bégin
> Archbishop of Quebec

Probably yielding to strong pressure from the bishops of Quebec, Mrs. Gérin-Lajoie resigned as president of the *Comité provincial pour le Suffrage féminin.* Mrs. Arthur Léger was elected to replace her and, on the English side, Mrs. E.T. Sampson succeeded Mrs. Walter Lyman. In 1927, disappointed by the apparent lack of zeal of the *Comité provincial*, Miss Idola Saint-Jean left our ranks and founded *l'Alliance canadienne pour le vote des femmes du Québec.* In *La Sphère féminine*, the official organ of her organization, Miss Saint-Jean gave as the reason for her defection of 1927, "The inactivity of the *Comité provincial* and its manifest failure to reach the working classes."[3] She claimed that her organization had deeper roots among the poorer classes and was composed entirely of French-speaking feminists. A curious attitude since Miss Saint-Jean taught French at McGill and had as friend and co-worker Mrs. John Scott, one of the acknowledged leaders of the temperance movement, which was supported chiefly by the English.

This division in the feminist forces did considerable damage to the work we had undertaken and delighted our enemies. Some people openly accused Miss Saint-Jean of being inflexible and of

54

presenting our demands with too much bitterness. I personally am convinced that she was sincere: her numerous articles on the status of women in Quebec, published in various papers and magazines, especially in *La Sphère féminine*, give abundant proof of this. Life sometimes offers curious surprises. Long after Miss Saint-Jean's death, I moved into a duplex on Mount Pleasant Street and was rearranging my basement locker when I encountered my landlady similarly occupied. Suddenly I noticed a pile of magazines that she was about to throw out. Imagine how amazed I was to find that it was a collection of *La Sphère féminine* and to learn that I was living in a house that had once belonged to Miss Saint-Jean. Recognizing their historical value, I immediately sent them off to the Montreal municipal library.

Between 1927 and 1929 several significant events occurred in the field of women's rights. The public was beginning to accept our ideas and several women's groups that had been engaged till then only in charitable work began to support the efforts of our committee. We decided to introduce a bill in favour of female suffrage at every session of the legislature. Many considered this a useless gesture since the Prime Minister and the Leader of the Opposition were still of one mind in their opposition to such a bill. Furthermore, Mr. Taschereau did not even see the use of putting it to a party vote. On the whole, however, we considered that repeating our demand each year would be an excellent way to obtain publicity and to influence public opinion in our favour. At each session, a different member of the Legislative Assembly introduced our bill–always an act of courage since the cause was lost in advance.

So on the 19th of February, 1927, the first such occasion in the history of our province, Victor Marchand, a member of the Legislative Assembly, introduced a bill to grant provincial suffrage to women. The members of the two parties defeated it by a vote of fifty-one to thirteen. This was only the beginning, the first of fourteen court-appearances before our peers in which we – mothers, wives, and sisters – played the role of defendants before a tribunal composed entirely of men. Often certain members even went so far as to reply to our requests with jeers, vulgarities, or cutting remarks before bringing down their verdict of curt rejection.

After a complete reorganization of the *Comité*, it was decided that a single person should assume its direction. I was elected president and the following year our association was incorporated as *La Ligue des Droits de la Femme*, a name more closely corresponding to the facts, since henceforth our activities would no longer be limited to obtaining provincial suffrage but would extend to include any legal, domestic, and social questions. We believed that obtaining the provincial vote was not the only reform needed, since at that period almost all the liberal professions were closed to women; teachers, as I mentioned earlier, received starvation wages (then a hundred and fifty to two hundred dollars a year); there was no legislation for the protection of children and there was even a law stipulating that no woman in the civil service should receive more than fifteen hundred dollars annually. Our Civil Code also needed amendment, for under our laws married women were considered to be minors under the authority of their husbands. They could belong to co-operative societies and devote their time and money to them but they had no voice in making decisions. So the battle was to be waged on all fronts at once.

For more than fourteen years I directed the fortunes of the *Ligue*, assisted by dedicated and well-informed people with whom it was always a pleasure to work even with our many problems. The fact that I was the wife of a federal Member of Parliament, who was Speaker of the House of Commons from 1936 to 1940, enabled me to make valuable political contacts that greatly aided our cause. As the mother of four children, I deprived anti-feminists of one of their favourite arguments: that most of the women who were seeking the right to vote were childless old harpies lacking any femininity. In this connection I remember a conversation with Prime Minister Taschereau, when he said to me with a smile, "Of course now that you're campaigning for the woman's vote, there'll be no question of your having any more children. But if such a thing should occur, I'd like to be godfather. If it's a boy we'll make him a bishop." "And if it's a girl," I retorted, "she'll be a suffragette." At that moment, as it happened, I was pregnant with my fourth child and, when she was born, my husband, who was federal member for Montmorency, which Mr. Taschereau represented in the Legislative Assembly, asked the Prime Minister if he wanted to keep his promise. So my youngest daughter, Renée, became the godchild of Mr. and Mrs. Taschereau. Thanks to the work of the *Ligue des Droits de la Femme*, she did not have to be a suffragette, and is today the happy mother of seven children.

The 27th of March, 1928 marked our second attempt to obtain the vote from our legislators. William Tremblay, the Conservative member for Maisonneuve, was our sponsor on this occasion. It was a memorable sitting of the Legislative Assembly; the galleries were crammed, almost entirely with women, and from the floor of the chamber came laughter and jokes. The members went at it to their heart's content until the Speaker was obliged to call the Assembly to order. After several speeches for and against the bill, one of the members moved that it be given the so-called six-months' hoist–in other words, due and proper burial. It was a free vote and the result: thirty-nine for the hoist, eleven against. And we witnessed the none too common spectacle of Prime Minister and Leader of the Opposition voting together. Evidently, anti-feminism didn't observe party lines.

The new defeat did not discourage us in the least but made us all the more determined to support our cause to the very end. A much appreciated sign of approval, along with tangible support, arrived soon afterwards in the form of two cheques, each of five hundred dollars, sent to Mrs. John Scott by Mrs. Carry Chapman Catt, leader of the suffrage movement in the United States. This money was turned over to the suffrage committee of the Montreal Women's Club and was used to conduct a vigorous publicity campaign which included the distribution of leaflets and the organization throughout the province of open meetings to inform the public. Another, rather more spectacular, form of publicity was inaugurated in Montreal and Quebec City. To the amazement of passers-by–for this was an unusual sight in those days–"sandwich-women" appeared on the main streets, carrying boldly lettered signs in support of women's suffrage. My memory isn't clear as to whether these ladies had any trouble with the police.

In 1929, I accompanied Mrs. Gérin-Lajoie, the president of the *Fédération nationale Saint-Jean-Baptiste* to present to the Committee of Public Bills the following proposed amendments to the Civil Code:

1. A clause dealing with the wages of married women.

2. A clause allowing women to become guardians and to play an effective role in family affairs.

3. The insertion into our Civil Code of Article 1422 of the *code Napoléon* to protect married women from the squandering of the family property by their husbands.

Mrs. Gérin-Lajoie's speech was remarkable and was later published as a pamphlet with the title, *Women and the Civil Code*. I in my turn presented the arguments likely to gain support for our position. During the trip Mrs. Gérin-Lajoie had told me of a particularly sad case that was one of the reasons for her interest in urging these reforms. It concerned a childless couple. The wife had managed to save ten thousand dollars out of the wages her husband paid her for her work as cashier in their business. In his middle years the husband began to sow wild oats and, to pay for his escapades, he asked his wife for half her savings. She refused, seeing the security of their old age threatened. The husband rushed furiously to the bank where the manager informed him that as head of the family he had a right not only to half but to the whole sum. Since he knew of the circumstances, the bank manager did not want to hand the money over to the husband, preferring to be taken to court. The case, unfortunately, was decided in the husband's favour.

Impressed by the seriousness of our arguments and by the complexity of the subject, Prime Minister Taschereau decided to appoint a government commission to revise the Civil Code according to the recommendations we had put forward. Various women's organizations insisted that women should be represented on the commission but needless to say this request was not granted. Shortly afterwards, I received the following letter:

> Dear Madame Casgrain,
>
> The Cabinet met this morning and appointed the Honourable Mr. Justice Dorion, Mr. Ferdinand Roy, Chief Magistrate of the Quebec District, and Messrs. Victorin Morin and Joseph Sirois, notaries, commissioners to study the section of the Civil Code that is concerned with marriage.
>
> I believe that you will have every reason to be satisfied with this choice. The four commissioners are all distinguished jurists who have practised actively and are well informed in this area.

I need not tell you that I shall instruct them to listen to all the representations that women may wish to make to them.

Yours very sincerely,
L. A. Taschereau

The Commissioners may have been learned jurists but it was evident that they were far from open to new ideas, as the following extract from their second report shows:

> Of more importance than equality is respect for order.
>
> This order demands frequent sacrifices of individual freedom. The marriage state creates certain duties and obligations for both the woman and the man and in their turn these duties and obligations create certain bonds. Each of us is free to establish a family or to retain our full independence; once the choice has been made, we are no longer free to reclaim the personal rights that the superior rights of the family have converted into duties.
>
> . . . We have heard mentioned the conditions of married women in other States or provinces; in our opinion this only weakens the present request. To follow the example of foreign legislation, which is inspired by principles in themselves alien to our moral education, would be to oppose the almost unanimous wish of the women of our province; above all, it would be, according to the spirit of our law, to turn our backs on the traditions that are still the most solid element in the order of our families. It is hardly the time, when the best-informed and clear-sighted experts, alarmed by what is happening in their societies, confess their admiration for what is happening in our society, for us to renounce the benefits of that discipline which is one of the surest indicators of our well-being.

To understand how important this Commission was, it would be well to recall the legal situation of married women in Quebec at this period. According to the law then in force, the couple were common as to property unless they had signed a notarised marriage contract providing otherwise. Without such a contract, the couple were subject to this law which, upon the husband's death, guaranteed to the wife half the property acquired by the husband during the marriage. During his lifetime, however, he alone had the right to administer all property – movable and immovable – of the family. He could therefore sell, transfer ownership, mortgage, or in any other way legally dispose of the common property without consulting his wife. These laws, which may have suited our families at a time when the great majority of the population was agricultural,

59

had become inadequate now that a good many women had an income of their own in the form of wages, bonuses, dividends, etc. This system gave rise to many abuses, when, for example, husbands, using their rights as administrators of all the family property and income, would receive their wives' wages every week and dispose of them quite legally.

Recommendations to the Dorion Commission proposed the following reforms to the Civil Code:

1. A reform in the administration of property when the husband and wife were common as to property;
2. The right of married women to dispose of their own wages;
3. The abolition, in the case of women who controlled their own property according to their marriage contract, of the need for them to obtain the authorization of their husband for the sale of immovable property;
4. An amendment to the Code concerning separation on grounds of adultery;
5. The repeal of the law that denied married women legal power.

Since I knew how important the decisions of the Dorion Commission would be to the women of Quebec, I asked a well-known jurist of the time, Eugène Lafleur, K.C., to plead our case. The presence of this eminent man impressed the Commissioners and they listened to his arguments with great attention. He admitted to me later in conversation that if he had realized the merits of our demands earlier, he would have put himself at our disposal long before that day. Mrs. Gérin-Lajoie presented her arguments in support of the necessary reforms with great energy and clarity, and Miss Idola Saint-Jean and Miss Irene Joly, the president of the *Association des femmes propriétaires*, also appeared before the Commission.

All these efforts were not entirely in vain. The Commission report, tabled in 1930, recommended sixteen amendments to the Civil Code, only a few of which were implemented by the legislature in 1931. One of the most important dealt with the question of the earnings of married women and amended article 1425a, which henceforth read as follows:

> Under all the systems and subject to the penalty of the nullity of
> any covenant to the contrary, the proceeds of the personal work

of the wife, the economies therefrom and the moveable or immoveable property acquired by her by investing same are reserved to the entire administration of the wife.

The wife may without authorization demand even before the courts the property so reserved and may alienate same by onerous title.

On the questions of wages, at least, the battle had been won. Not so in the matter of civil incapacity. The law continued to deny the married woman all legal power including the right to make contracts without the authorization of her husband. In addition, requests for a couple legally to live apart, could not be based upon the mutual consent of the spouses, but had to be presented for a very specific cause. The provisions of the Code read as follows:

ART. 187. A husband may demand a separation on the ground of his wife's adultery.
ART. 188. A wife may demand the separation on the ground of her husband's adultery if he keeps his concubine in their common habitation.

Everyone concerned about social justice instantly demanded that this state of affairs should cease, pointing out that such a reform had been introduced in France in 1884. The arguments against the double standard could be summarized as follows: "According to moral law, the fault is equal; according to civil law, it is—on one side as on the other—a violation of the duty of mutual fidelity to which husband and wife both submit and to which they are not bound in different degrees."

To these arguments based on sound logic, the second report of the Dorion Commission offered evasive replies in which false sentimentality had more place than reason:

Everyone should agree, we are told, that the moral fault is equal and that adultery is always an injury.

However, we do not believe that the law should be amended to the point of no longer distinguishing between the act of the man and that of the woman. Psychologically and socially, the distinction still continues to be necessary.

In principle, adultery can be as sharp a wound for a woman as for a man; but whatever may be said, everyone knows that, in fact, the wound to the heart of the wife is not generally as severe as the wound to the husband who has been deceived by his wife.

It would be difficult to explain by pure reason this difference in feeling but it is true that "the heart has its reasons that the mind cannot know." . . .

It is not equal because it is a fault that is often advantageous to forgive and *to the heart of woman forgiveness is naturally easier.* Those around her display pity and kindness. The husband, however, though he may suffer quite as much, receives no sympathy for the injury done to his family; the infidelity of his wife exposes him to *ridicule.*

The offence is not entirely equal, for the adultery of the wife may have other and particularly aggravating consequences. Their common life may become impossible because, legally, the husband cannot disavow any child born to his wife during their marriage.

Are the children he is rearing his own? He is the only one of the two who can be made to suffer by this question. And the child of doubtful parentage, when the husband knows of the fault of his wife, is a constant reminder of the blow—and prevents the wound from closing over with time.

Undoubtedly *the husband can also have children outside the marriage;* but his wife does not rear them.

So if morally the fault is equal, it is not of equal consequence.

This judgment on a question of such gravity by such eminent members of our magistracy would be ridiculous if it were not so tragic.

In conclusion, it may be said that while the Dorion report brought a few amendments to our Civil Code, it did not go very far. The Commission claimed that the law has changed little because women are still the same and on the whole do not want any radical changes. The reforms requested, the report continued, "only illustrate the incontestable *value* of our laws and their beneficial influence upon the lot of women. That is why certain demands should, in our opinion, be firmly rejected. Either they have been proposed to remedy an evil that is not really an evil, or they propose for a real, although isolated, misfortune a remedy that would not be effective. In either case the reform requested would be harmful. For though the laws are normally based on customs, these laws may have in their turn a harmful influence upon customs. They can thus engender an evil or aggravate a particular evil by generalizing it."

Between these lines it is easy to observe the scornful and haughty attitude of our masculine elite towards women. A few years later I met Mr. Justice Ferdinand Roy and naturally told him of our disappointment in the report of the Commission on the civil rights of women. The learned judge had to admit that the Commission had not gone far enough in proposing reforms to the Civil Code.

In spite of our disappointment, my colleagues and I decided to continue our struggles on all fronts. Women had obtained the vote in most of the other provinces but they still had no representative in the Senate. This fact had been drawn to public attention by a resolution adopted unanimously by the Federated Women's Institutes of Canada during their first convention in 1919. At a meeting chaired by Judge Emily Murphy, a resolution was drawn up to be presented to Prime Minister Borden, asking that he open the doors of the Upper House to Canadian women. The National Council of Women and several other organizations made similar representations. Two years later, in 1921, Mrs. John Scott, president of the Montreal Women's Club and well-known for her outspokenness and indomitable courage, asked Arthur Meighen, now the Prime Minister, to appoint Emily Murphy to the Senate as soon as there was a vacancy in Alberta; she had been appointed to the bench after a very active struggle to obtain female suffrage in that province. The mounting pressure of favourable public opinion resulted in Meighen's promise during the 1921 general election that he would take the steps necessary to obtain the admission of women to the Upper House. In 1922 the new Prime Minister, MacKenzie King, also expressed sympathy with the idea and even went as far as to say that he would, if need be, have the British North America Act amended. Despite all these fine words, time passed and nothing happened.

In 1927 Emily Murphy decided that there was nothing to be expected from all these politicians. She consulted several lawyers and finally Mr. Justice William Nassau Ferguson drew her attention to Article 60 of the Supreme Court Act, which made it possible for five people to petition the Government for an order-in-council requesting an interpretation from the Supreme Court of a constitutional point in the BNA Act. Since these steps would involve a great deal of expense, Mrs. Murphy wished to know whether the Government would agree to offer financial assistance. The Crown replied in the affirmative and Mrs. Murphy chose four other well known women to act with her.

She first approached Mrs. Nellie McClung, a noted author and journalist, an excellent speaker, and an ardent feminist, through whose efforts the women of Alberta and Manitoba had obtained the provincial vote as early as 1916. It is told that she used the occasion of her fiftieth wedding anniversary to refute the argument of those who claimed that women's procurement of political rights would destroy the life of the home; her own marital happiness was surely proof to the contrary. Mrs. Murphy also recruited the Honourable Irene Parlby, a minister in the Alberta legislature since 1921; Mrs. Louise McKinney, also a member of the Alberta legislature; and Mrs. Henrietta Muir Edwards, a member of the legislation committee of the National Council of Women and the author of two pamphlets on the legal status of women in Canada and in Alberta.

On the 27th of August, 1928, the Governor-General-in-Council petitioned the Supreme Court of Canada to obtain a ruling as to whether the word "person" in Section 24 of the BNA Act included "female persons." On the following 14th of March the petition reached the Supreme Court for argument.[4] The Honourable Lucien Cannon, the solicitor general, appeared for the Canadian government. Some years before, while a member of the Quebec Legislative Assembly, Mr. Cannon had introduced a bill to obtain the admission of women to the Bar. Now he was placed in the opposing camp. His opponent was Newton Wesley Rowell, an eminent Toronto attorney who in 1916-17, while Leader of the Liberal Opposition of Ontario, had been a strong advocate of women's suffrage. Mr. Rowell also represented the Alberta government, which supported the petition of the five women. Quebec sent Charles Lanctot as special counsel to support the Honourable Lucien Cannon. It is regrettable to note that once again it was the representatives of Quebec who argued the negative side. Mr. Rowell's factum was short and readily comprehensible. It stipulated, in general, that the word "person" applied to men and women alike. The argument of the Crown was at least six times as long and included numerous references to laws and customs going back to Roman times. Besides supporting Mr. Cannon's argu-

64

ment, Mr. Lanctot maintained that there was no justification whatever for women to take part in public life. The conclusions of the Supreme Court were brought down by Mr. Chief Justice Anglin on the 24th of April, 1928. He stated that the Court shared the historical viewpoint in this matter and that, on account of women's civil incapacity under common law in 1867 when the BNA Act was adopted, women were not eligible to be senators.[5]

Though profoundly disappointed, Mrs. Murphy and her friends did not lose courage and decided to appeal the decision to the Privy Council in London. They let the 1928 parliamentary sessions pass, still hoping that government action would make their appeal unnecessary. For had not the Honourable Ernest Lapointe, the minister of justice, said in the House of Commons on the very day of the judgment that the Government would immediately take the steps necessary to have Article 24 of the BNA Act amended. There was fear, of course, that one of the provinces–above all Quebec–might raise objections to any such change. And even if the amendment passed the Commons, it could still meet stronger opposition in the Senate.

So the 1928 session concluded with the promise of the Minister of Justice not being fulfilled. Encouraged by their lawyers, Judge Emily Murphy and her friends decided to proceed with their appeal to the Privy Council. Illogical as it may seem, the Minister of Justice once more offered the appellants his entire co-operation. On the 20th of November, 1928, an order-in-council gave the five women permission to appeal to the judicial committee of the Privy Council. The Alberta government again strongly supported the petition and even delegated its solicitor-general, the Honourable J.F. Lymburn, to support Mr. Rowell. On the 15th of June, 1929, the appellants were delighted to learn that Prime Minister Taschereau was withdrawing his province from the litigation.

What is remarkable and disturbing about this struggle was the essentially conservative attitude of the provincial government. It is clear also that the greatest enemies of Quebec women were the representatives they had helped send to Ottawa; yet these same women had most to suffer from this usurpation of their rights as citizens. This was only one aspect of a greater problem, that of liberalizing the mentality of the people of Quebec.

On the 28th of July, 1929, in London began the proceedings that were to decide finally whether women should be considered "persons." For long hours, learned advocates discussed the various aspects of the case before the judicial committee presided over by Lord Chancellor Sankey. When he brought down his verdict on the 18th of October, he gave thousands of Canadian women a new sense of dignity. He stated:

> ...Their lordships have come to the conclusion that the word person includes members of the male and female sex, and that therefore the question propounded by the Governor General must be answered in the affirmative, and that women are eligible to be summoned and become members of the Senate of Canada.

I need not describe the joy with which Mrs. Murphy and her companions received this news. More than thirteen years had passed since that day in a little courtroom in Edmonton when Judge Emily Murphy had been bluntly told by an attorney that in the eyes of the law she was not a person. Prime Minister Mackenzie King seemed happy about the decision and added that if the women had lost their case, he would have had the BNA Act amended. One cannot help recalling that he had not dared do this earlier when the Supreme Court had pronounced against the eligibility of women to the Senate of Canada.

On a beautiful sunny morning in 1930 the Government in Ottawa announced the appointment of Mrs. Cairine Wilson as the first woman senator. A woman of independent means, and an ardent Liberal, Mrs. Wilson was the daughter of Senator Robert Mackay and the mother of eight children. Without wishing to belittle or underrate her diligence and competence in any way, I admit that I have always infinitely regretted that such women as Emily Murphy, Nellie McClung or Irene Parlby were not chosen. No one can deny that their perseverance and courage opened the doors of the Senate to Canadian women. There is a commemorative plaque to these five women in the Parliament in Ottawa, the only tribute that was ever paid to them, and not one of them ever crossed the threshold of the lofty chamber of the Upper House to sit as a senator.

VI

Once More unto the Breach . . .

I had long observed the work accomplished in the rest of Canada and in the United States by the Junior League. In French Canada, however, there was no movement of this sort. As the doors of the universities were scarcely open to our girls and remunerative work was frowned upon, most of them had no specific occupation and did not know how to fill their time while they waited for marriage. As a result, some of them turned to the Junior League.

Thus the idea came to me that I should organize a group that would give our young women the opportunity to become involved in social work, since problems in this field were becoming more and more acute. I realized that public opinion would be more favourable if I formed a committee of women somewhat older than myself who were already well known in charity work. A meeting was held at the Ritz Carlton Hotel in 1926 and the new organization was given the name of the *Ligue de la Jeunesse féminine*. It goes without saying that there were some difficult moments, especially when the *Ligue* decided not to have a chaplain. Several unions and most of the Catholic associations had their chaplains and a large section of the population found our attitude scandalous. We, for our part, considered that such an appointment was unnecessary since our members had already received the upbringing they required to meet their responsibilities.

The *Ligue's* first president, Hélène Grenier, an intelligent and cultivated girl and a trained librarian had a constitution drawn up, based largely on that of the Junior League. The members hoped to use radio, press, and social contacts to reach the various levels of society and make them aware of the need for more effective social action. Shortly afterwards a branch was set up in Quebec City under the presidency of Martha St-Laurent, the daughter of Louis St-Laurent, who became Prime Minister of Canada in 1946. In 1936 the *Ligue* founded a school for crippled children, named after Cardinal Villeneuve who was strongly in favour of this project. The *Ligue* has been functioning now for many years and its annual ball, *le Bal des petits souliers,* is still an important event in the social life of Montreal.

Meanwhile the struggle to obtain the provincial vote and the admission of women to the Bar and certain other liberal professions still remained to be won. In 1930 a new attempt was made and Oscar Drouin agreed to introduce a bill dealing with these two points. Once again the women met defeat. Probably to tease me, Robert Taschereau, the Prime Minister's son who was at that time member for Bellechasse, showed me a note from his father. Robert had asked whether he should vote for the admission of women to the Bar. "Vote against it," the Prime Minister replied. "There are enough lawyers already."

We increased our efforts and later that year a Liberal M.L.A. Mr. Irénée Vautrin, introduced a new bill demanding women's suffrage. It happened to be the Honourable Alexandre Taschereau's birthday and the members of the *Ligue des Droits de la Femme* arranged to have a bouquet of sixty-three red roses placed on the Prime Minister's desk. While there was some irony in this choice of flowers with thorns, we felt that the gesture showed that we were still above being petty. The members of the *Alliance pour le vote des femmes du Québec* refused to join us in this symbolic gesture, declaring that they had no intention of being friendly to one who, while boasting of being a Liberal, was so clearly the enemy of the weaker sex. We for our part believed that it is always harder to catch flies with vinegar than with honey. Here is the letter Mr. Taschereau wrote to me on this occasion:

Quebec, March 6, 1930

Dear Madame Casgrain,

I am sorry that I did not see you after the sitting yesterday to thank you for the superb bouquet of flowers you sent me.

You are "a good sport" and I do not deserve flowers. I thank you with all my heart. I should also like to congratulate you on your personal success. You have opened a breach in our ranks which we shall now have to repair!

Sincerely yours,
L.A. Taschereau

In support of his bill, Mr. Vautrin delivered an eloquent speech, which won him the encouragement of several other ministers, among them the Honourable Athanase David, the provincial secretary. In 1922, his father, Senator L.O. David, had introduced an amendment to the Women's Suffrage Act in the Senate that would have granted the vote to women only when they reached the age of thirty. One might wonder why he believed that, when they reached that age, women should suddenly be imbued with wisdom and knowledge. Athanase David's brilliant speech on this occasion has remained in the memory of those who were present and has its place in the history of our province. He went beyond the question of female suffrage and urged his colleagues to become aware, before it was too late, of the profound changes taking place in our society. He maintained that placing the vote in the hands of women would in no way disturb the equilibrium of our society. Much more grave, in his opinion, and more likely to cause social upheavals, was the problem of the numerous mothers of families who were forced to leave home and children each morning to work for starvation wages in the factories in order to balance the family budget.

The single discordant note of the day was a stupid tirade from Mr. Ephraim Bédard who maintained that the adoption of such a law would destroy home life in our province. Rather impolitely he suggested that the bill be sent to committee not for six months but for nine, a proposal he couched in somewhat unparliamentary terms. Great roars of laughter greeted this alleged witticism, an indication of the low calibre of some of our representatives.

Despite the eloquence and sincerity of Messrs. Vautrin and David, the bill was rejected by a vote of forty-four to twenty-four. This result, however, was better than that of the previous year and encouraged us to persevere in our efforts.

In the federal election of 1930 Miss Idola Saint-Jean stood as a candidate in Dorion-Saint-Denis. She wished more to open up new fields, and had no illusions about her chances of being elected. Nevertheless, she managed to obtain about three thousand votes. For the first time in our province, a woman had been a candidate for a federal seat.

A little later the *Ligue des Droits de la Femme*, supported by Miss Irene Joly, the president of the *Association des Femmes propriétaires*, recommended to the provincial government that it amend the charter of Montreal to permit married women who owned property to vote in municipal elections. This proposal was accepted by the Montreal City Council but was turned down by the Quebec Government, which had jurisdiction over municipalities. The measure was not finally adopted until February, 1932. The anti-feminists probably saw in advance that as the result of this change in the Municipal Act, the names of a host of women property-owners would be included on the voters' lists, replacing those of their husbands who had possessed the right to vote only because of the property qualifications of their wives.

In 1931 Irénée Vautrin, a Liberal, sponsored our fifth attempt to obtain the vote in provincial elections. He was supported by two Conservative members, Martin Fisher, the member for Huntington, and General C.A. Smart, the member for Westmount. All who spoke in favour of the measure emphasized the increasingly important role of women in the economic life of the nation. Mr. Fisher declared that the provincial authorities were demeaning the women of Quebec by this refusal to recognize their rights. Another member pointed out that the impressive number of women who had voted in the 1930 federal election showed very clearly that they were concerned with the political problems of the day.

Everyone, however, did not view matters in this light. A young Liberal M.L.A., Amédée Caron of Hull, attacked the bill in a violent speech and so heatedly that one felt he was seeking what might be considered some rather dubious publicity, for the Prime Minister listened to him with a satisfied smile. Unfortunately such an attitude was often assumed to curry favour with the leader rather than from any real conviction. The bill was once again defeated but the idea was gaining ground, as was shown by the vote of the ministers, which was now equally divided–five in favour, five against.

We of the *Ligue* realized the importance of gaining more support from the public, for it was evident that those for whose interests we were fighting–the women of Quebec–did not always appreciate our efforts. We had lived for years in the incredibly odd position of being able to express our opinion on national or international questions in federal elections, without having a voice in solving problems closer to home, such as education and health. It was interesting to note the contrast in the attitudes of federal and provincial candidates during election campaigns. Federal candidates increased their attentions to women voters and flattered them at meetings to solicit their vote. The reverse was true during provincial elections; when we asked candidates to support important social measures, they shrugged impatiently or ignored us, often without even bothering to be polite.

But to return to the publicity campaign of the *Ligue,* the CBC had just been established and, understanding the importance of this new medium, we managed to obtain a regular program called *Fémina.* We thought that it would be a good idea to have male voices heard supporting us and so a number of young lawyers and businessmen agreed to be our spokesmen. Several of those who defended women's suffrage over the air because they considered it a necessary contribution to true democracy later became learned judges.

In 1932 Dr. Anatole Plante, a Liberal member, entered the fray in his turn by consenting to sponsor the famous and much-discussed bill. This time the debate took a particularly disagreeable form. Certain members of the Legislative Assembly, in fine fettle that day, prolonged the discussion for almost two hours, each firing off his little speech, most of them marked by real vulgarity. They seemed to have chosen Miss Saint-Jean as their special target, directing remarks at her that were in the worst possible taste. Two members particularly excelled in the fine art of boorishness, the representatives of Lévis and Laval, the latter going so far as to offer Miss Saint-Jean his trousers. At times, even misfortune can be useful, for this disgraceful debate aroused the indignation of the public. Disgusted by the tone of these deliberations, many people began to take a more serious interest in our cause.

The following year, on the 22nd of February, 1933, Dr. Plante again consented to sponsor our bill, which was defeated this time by a vote of fifty-five to twenty. However, the tone of the debate had changed and the matter was treated more seriously. Visibly irritated by the incomprehension of his colleagues, Dr. Plante said, more or less in these words, "French Canadians have one great fault. They are smug and so convinced of their own perfection that they forget to look at what is happening around them." He then presented these arguments in favour of women's suffrage:

1. There need be no fear of our parliaments being invaded by women members.
2. The presence of a few women in government would lend the Legislative Assembly more distinction and might induce some members to pay more attention to the sittings of the House.
3. The women would be as interested in politics and would make at least as much use of their vote as the men, only 77 per cent of whom voted in the last general election.

Dr. Ernest Poulin replied in these terms:

1. Has the women's vote, where it exists, brought improvements in political and social conditions?
2. Are the other provinces of Canada better off since the women have voted?
3. Giving the vote to women would completely wreck our social order.
4. Female suffrage is contrary to the spirit of the Catholic Church and would accomplish no useful purpose.

Another equally narrow-minded member, Mr. A. Legault, expressed his fears for the social order and the dangers of its being overthrown and added: "This female vote is premature and dangerous because of the difficult times in which we are living."

Utterances of this sort show how stupid and ignorant some of the representatives of the people were. The women of Quebec had been voting in federal elections since 1919, they had voted at the beginning of the nineteenth century, and yet the catastrophes certain members now feared had not occurred. Such ultra-conservatism was unfortunately shared by too many women. In 1933, *Canada Français* published an article signed by Mrs. A. Croff in which she stated: "French-Canadian women are quite indifferent to politics," and went on to say that women "can influence the decisions and wishes of men without acting like men themselves."

A study of the parish of Saint-Denis-sur-Richelieu by the sociologist Horace Miners indicated the same viewpoint among the women. He stated that the latter, the wives of farmers in the region, were not in the least interested in politics, which they considered "too dirty for women to be bothered about in their homes." Single women showed a more marked concern with politics—no doubt, he said, because this was the only means they possessed to express their convictions.

The opinions of Mrs. Croff and Mr. Miners were in complete opposition to my own. While accompanying my husband on several election campaigns in rural areas, I had observed the presence of a great many women at the various meetings, all displaying interest in the questions raised. Moreover, many electors had told us that they wished to consult their wives before opting for one party or the other because the latter often had very sound views on the problems of the day. Of course prejudices were deeply rooted at this period, even among some people who had a certain amount of education but were still affected by the general tenor of our society.

The influence of the clergy was very strong and extended to every sphere of family and community life. In the pulpit or in the pages of such journals as *L'Action catholique,* the religious leaders pronounced on all these matters. Their opposition to women's suffrage was not only based upon a false interpretation of religious principles but also owed much to that secular atavism, expressed by a need for domination and a sense of superiority, that is found in varying degrees among a certain male element of our society.

The years went by. In 1934 it was the turn of Dr. Gaspard Fauteux, the Liberal member for Saint-Jacques and later Lieutenant Governor of the province, to present the female suffrage bill. On this occasion, the women of the delegation that went down to Quebec City again noted that our radio publicity was beginning to make itself felt, for the tone of the debate had again improved. Even so, we were defeated for the eighth time. The prejudices of the Legislative Assembly continued to prevail over common sense. It seemed to those of us who supported this liberal measure that the more favourable public opinion became to our cause, the more our opponents in the Legislative Assembly tried through ridicule to belittle or diminish the importance of our work.

Our sustained and courageous efforts were attracting the attention of our fellow-women in other provinces. It was at about this time, if my memory serves, that we received a message from the National Federation of Liberal Women, of which Senator Cairine Wilson was president, expressing their sympathy for the lack of political power of the women of Quebec.

Our attempt in 1935, was notable chiefly for a statement from Robert Bachand: "Since cigarettes and cocktails are no longer masculine prerogatives," he said, "the least the ladies can do is leave politics to the gentlemen." Apparently the majority of his colleagues were of the same opinion for we suffered our ninth failure.

During this same year, 1935, the suffragette group of Quebec made a gesture that from our present vantage point might tend to make us smile. His Majesty King George V was celebrating his silver jubilee and Miss Idola Saint-Jean conceived the ambitious project of involving our sovereign in the feminist cause. Some ten thousand signatures were collected for a petition to be presented to the King. It should be noted that we were then the only white women among his subjects who were deprived of the right to vote, whereas a century before we had been the only ones who possessed it. A duly qualified intermediary had to be found to present the petition. As might have been expected, the Quebec government refused us this service but a private citizen who was travelling to London undertook to deliver the document to Buckingham Palace. We have never known whether it reached its destination but our chief aim had been to attract attention. Since the whole affair received a great deal of publicity, we were satisfied with the result.

VII

Prejudices in Retreat

The struggle for the right to vote did not leave me indifferent to the other problems of my country. Like the rest of Canada, the province had been plunged into a deep economic depression beginning towards the end of 1929. The Quebec government, Liberal in principle but increasingly reactionary in practice, had been in power since 1896. It facilitated the establishment of major industries by ceding them land and granting them tax exemptions. Furthermore, industry as well as the natural riches of the province were largely in foreign hands. French-Canadian workers were wretchedly paid and were usually obliged to adopt English as their working language. During election campaigns, Prime Minister Taschereau appealed to foreign industrialists, urging them to establish themselves in Quebec where, he said, "Wages are low and the population docile." Patronage was rife in the Quebec government and many civil servants received regular pay cheques without ever appearing for work; most of them, needless to say, were relatives of those in power. Though aware of this, the people remained passive. The enormous hold of the clergy in some parishes scarcely encouraged action among those who were aware of the need for reform and ready to act. In some places, the prevailing attitude could be summed up in these words by Léopold Richer: " ... the ignorance of rural labour and the daily battle against the forest, ... the rags of poverty, misery, hunger, and cold; our ancestors had to accept all these and we too must accept them if we are to remain faithful to our faith, our language, and our laws."[1]

Young girls would ring my doorbell and offer their services for ridiculous wages or even free in exchange for food and lodging. When I travelled with Pierre during the 1930 election campaign,

I observed the terrible poverty in rural districts. While my husband went down to the outlying parts of his riding–Havre-Saint-Pierre and Sept-Îles–I remained at La Malbaie. Before he left, he had warned Calixte Cormier, his organizer in that part of the riding, of the danger of holding a political meeting at La Malbaie, where feelings were running high chiefly because of the election. Despite this advice, Mr. Cormier organized a meeting at the local classical college. The hall was packed. Paul Gouin, then at the beginning of his political career, was present. When it came his turn to speak, he announced that he had just returned from Europe; a wag wondered why he ever came back. Indescribable pandemonium ensued and, in an attempt to calm the audience, I was lifted onto a table. "My friends," I said, "since you don't want to listen to speeches, we're going to sing," and I struck up *O Canada*. With the last notes, the uproar resumed and someone cut off the electricity, plunging the college into total darkness and putting a rather distressing end to the gathering.

During another meeting, this time at Baie-Saint-Paul, the federal minister, Lucien Cannon, who had come to help Pierre in his campaign, also had to address a tempestuous audience. Right in front of him sat a toothless old man who heckled him continually. Losing patience, Cannon said finally, "My friend, if you want people to understand you, go and get yourself some teeth." The old man replied humorously, "What would be the use? There's nothing to eat." There was a great roar of laughter. Such incidents show how quick-witted are our people but also how wretched were the conditions in which they lived.

As the general public became more receptive to the idea of women voting, election campaigns, which were rather rough in those days, became less violent. One reason for this, I suspect, was the number of women at election meetings where their presence seemed to have a calming effect. Pierre was re-elected but the Liberals lost their majority in Parliament and Mackenzie King was replaced by R.B. Bennett.

I always admired my husband's attitude in the face of defeat. A realist and a dedicated public servant, he avoided making promises that would be impossible to keep but devoted himself to improving conditions for his constituents. It was during his mandate that the first air-mail service began between Sept-Îles, Havre-Saint-Pierre, and Quebec City. He also had a dock built at Baie Comeau, today an important port with a population of more than seven thousand. His constituents often came to see him when they happened to be in Montreal. One morning our doorbell rang at about seven o'clock. A maid hastened to answer it and soon a strong odour of *tabac canadien* spread through the house. Throwing on some clothes, my husband and I went down to the living room where we found a resident of Petite-Rivière-St-François puffing away on his pipe. He had sailed up to Montreal and come to say hello to his member of parliament at what was to him a perfectly normal hour to make a visit. While we were chatting, two of our children came in to greet him before leaving for school. Curious, he asked how many youngsters we had. "Four," I answered proudly. He looked at me in astonishment. "Is that all? I've got twelve." And his face clearly showed how much superior he felt.

In the atmosphere of political instability and economic chaos of the early 1930s, Paul Gouin invited a group of friends to the Reform Club, a club almost exclusively frequented by Liberals in Montreal. After a friendly dinner, he said, "There's talk of starting a new political movement within the Liberal party." This was the beginning of *Action libérale*. Paul Gouin had often invited various young Liberals to his home—among others François Badaud, Gérard Parizeau, Léon Gérin-Lajoie, Séraphin Vachon, Roger Ouimet, Calixte Cormier, Jean Martineau, and Fred Monk—all of whom were interested in carrying out reforms within the Liberal party. While they discussed politics, the wives played bridge. I was quite interested in what they said and remember the rather mocking way the other ladies would say between hands, "She doesn't play cards and the men are willing to let her sit in on their meetings." Indeed, I was often present but, as I wished to learn, I spoke little and listened a great deal.

For more than a year before the actual founding of *Action libérale*, I used to entertain informally every Monday evening, and gradually various political cliques formed. Prime Minister Taschereau, who was perfectly aware that I considered his government reactionary, told Pierre one day that he wanted these gatherings to cease, but my husband did not think it advisable to comply. Needless to say

77

that those present did not always agree. Several of my guests had very liberal ideas whereas others wanted to maintain French Canadians in their ancestral traditions. Paul Gouin's opinions lay somewhere between these two extremes. He was a charming and cultivated man and an excellent speaker, but showed a certain hesitancy and too often tended to be indecisive. He was influenced, I believe, by the theories of Father Papin Archambault's *École sociale populaire*; in other words he was not so far to the left as many of the others but was still a reformer.

I remember well several others in the group. Calixte Cormier, a young lawyer, was a tireless worker and extraordinarily dynamic. The son of a poor family in Sherbrooke, he had had to earn the money for his education. He had witnessed the frustrations of his close friend, Dr. Émilien Noël, who had tried without success to negotiate with the provincial government for the building of a hospital in Sherbrooke. He had been very disappointed by the weaknesses of the Liberal party and it was this, I believe, that influenced him to become one of the founders of *Action libérale*. I knew him very well since he was a member of my husband's law firm and often helped him during election campaigns. His sudden death at thirty-nine was deeply regretted by his friends who were shocked, as were many others, by Duplessis' comment that Heaven had come to his aid by removing one of his most dangerous enemies.

Another regular guest at my Monday evenings was the lawyer Jean Martineau, a man of extremely liberal ideas and absolute honesty, who was never afraid to declare and defend his positions. A member of the Reform Club, he was often shocked by what he saw there and seldom hesitated to say so. He was one of Paul Gouin's chief supporters and had the temperament of a leader though without the necessary tact. His cold and logical way of thinking and his tendency to express his opinions with scarcely a thought for the impression he might be giving, made him many enemies. A few years after the collapse of *Action libérale nationale*, he returned to the Liberal fold, where he soon carved himself out an enviable position. He became *bâtonnier* of the Quebec Bar and eventually an Appeal Court judge. But as this sort of work was little to his liking, he resigned after a few years and returned to private practice. During the 1950s he represented Gaspé Copper Mines in their celebrated case against the steelworkers during the Murdockville strike. He was later appointed chairman of the Canada Council, where he was able to put his great qualities to work.

Roger Ouimet, also a lawyer and today a Superior Court judge, was another very active member of the group that founded *Action libérale*. I knew him when he was courting a young friend of mine, the daughter of Ernest Lapointe, who often used to spend a few weeks with me, and whom he later married. I have always been grateful to him as one of the Liberals who aided the cause of women's suffrage. It was also through his work that the Quebec nurses obtained their charter under Duplessis.

As well, there was the federal member of parliament, Édouard Lacroix, a very intelligent, liberal-minded man, an ardent admirer of Ernest Lapointe, and one of his faithful supporters. Very popular in Beauce, where he was born, he had been elected without difficulty to represent that riding in the House of Commons. While engaged in the lumber business, he had witnessed many abuses which he deplored. As a result, he had often clashed with the Taschereau government over the question of timber limits, and advocated wide reforms. He was of great assistance to *Action libérale* in its beginning.

The movement gained strength and on the 28th of July, 1934, the manifesto of *Action libérale* appeared in the French-language press. Among other reforms, this wide-ranging program proposed the encouragement of small industry, settling new areas in the province, assistance to agriculture by increased production for local markets, economic control of the province by French Canadians, and government action to restrain the trusts. In the area of social welfare it recommended the restoration of a social, economic, and political order based on the family, the protection of children, laws to regulate hours of work and minimum wages, sickness and disability insurance, and old age pensions. It also advocated a program of rural assistance, including electrification and increased farm subsidies, and a complete reform of the electoral system.

Some of the proposed economic measures, such as land-settlement and the encouragement of small industry, in my opinion, showed the Quebec nationalist spirit at its narrowest and pettiest; to try to return to small industry in the middle of the twentieth century seemed to me impractical and dangerous. As for land-settlement, I had heard workers from Abitibi tell of the misery and starvation of the settlers in that area – former city-dwellers with no farming experience – and I was of the opinion that such a "return to the soil" offered no solution to the problem of unemployment. While our people supported these measures, heavy industry was passing increasingly into the hands of English Canadians or foreigners. I thought also that there should have been more emphasis placed upon the importance of trade-union action, for though American and English-Canadian workers were becoming increasingly organized, those who tried to do so here were eyed with disfavour.

When our clergy began to realize that they could not stop the workers from joining trade unions, they established the Catholic syndicates to prevent our people from becoming members of the international federations which had already organized workers in the construction, electrical and some other industries. Since public opinion was quite willing to accept the existence of such business and professional associations as the Canadian Manufacturers Association, the Chamber of Commerce, and the Bar, why should it have balked at associations of workers? But at that time, any question of reform was considered dangerous and leading inevitably to communism. Some of our more narrow-minded clergy used every possible means to preserve the customs of bygone times – an attitude that still exists in some places.

In 1935, *La Province* was founded as the official organ of *Action libérale*. The paper appeared only from time to time because of the limited financial resources of the group and the expenses of their Sunday radio broadcasts. Séraphin Vachon was the editor and contributors were not paid. Advertisers were scarce, for the principles of the new party were frightening at the time and many people hesitated to identify themselves publicly with such a reform program.

Taschereau announced a provincial election for the 25th of November, 1935. The old saying that elections are not won by prayers once again proved true. "That was why," Jean Martineau recounts, "a meeting was held at Lucien Dansereau's house in the country. There were about thirty of us. Fred Monk was there and even some people from Quebec City. At that time we still didn't want to add the word *nationale* to our name. We had the impression that the Conservative Party was trying to swallow us. A few months before the election, there had been an agreement between the Conservatives under Maurice Duplessis and *Action libérale* under Paul Gouin that we should make a common front against the Liberals. I believe it was then that the word *nationale* was added to the name of our group so that it would indicate, on one side, reforms of liberal inspiration and, on the other, Quebec nationalism." It is clear that the presence of a number of Quebec nationalists in the *Action libérale nationale* caused many people to break with the group. The Montrealers, such as Fred Monk, Jean Martineau, and Calixte Cormier, were, above all, liberal reformers, whereas those from Quebec City, as Dr. Philippe Hamel and Ernest Grégoire, were primarily nationalists.

In an attempt to meet the growing popularity of the ALN head on, Taschereau created a Ministry of Industry and Commerce and appointed Ernest Lapointe, who was then a member of the Opposition in Ottawa and had often been very irritated by Taschereau's attitude, chairman of the Hydro Commission. All the young Liberals of the ALN were great admirers of Ernest Lapointe, although they wished at times that he would be more forceful. We met him shortly after his appointment and I remember being scolded by my husband because to Mr. Lapointe's question, "Aren't you going to congratulate me?" I had replied, "No, because when you start by giving way in small things, you are soon giving way in big things." Pierre thought me too young to express such opinions.

The results of the 1935 election were as follows: forty-seven Liberals, one Independent Liberal and forty-two *Union nationale* which included twenty-six ALN. Taschereau remained in power and scheduled a sitting of the Legislative Assembly for the end of March, 1936. A rather stormy session followed, and gradually it became clear that Duplessis was the real leader of the anti-Taschereau group and the future prime minister of Quebec. An incident during this session showed once again the inferior position assigned to women in our society and the sort of hostility they had to face. A Liberal member, J.-A. Francoeur, wanted, like everyone else, to provide some solution to the terrible problem of unemployment and could think of nothing better than to introduce a bill to prohibit women from engaging in any work except farming, cooking, and domestic service. Even Mr. Taschereau opposed the bill as being impractical. He was not ready to refuse women the right to work for others to earn their living, though he still opposed their entering public life. Mr. Francoeur's bill received only sixteen votes. Still it seems incredible that sixteen of our legislators should have supported such a measure.

Throughout the session, the real battle was being waged in the corridors of the Legislature and elsewhere. The coffers of the ALN were empty and its forces badly organized. Its members fell one by one into Duplessis' net, thanks chiefly to the funds at his disposal with which he helped them pay their election debts. Gouin's group was reduced to only a few friends. It must be said that his weaknesses as a leader were at least partially responsible for this situation.

After a series of unfortunate events and tumultuous debates, Taschereau resigned with his entire cabinet on the 11th of June, 1936, and the Legislative Assembly dissolved. His Minister of Agriculture, Adélard Godbout, formed a caretaker government. A week later Paul Gouin announced that the ALN was withdrawing from the *Union nationale* and would continue to oppose "the two old parties, both of which were conservative and monopolistic, that of the Honourable Adélard Godbout and that of Mr. Duplessis." Almost all the ALN members of the Legislative Assembly chose to remain with the *Union nationale*. A month before the election, which was held in the late summer of 1936, the ALN announced that it was leaving politics and would concentrate its efforts upon education. Paul Gouin seems to have made this decision entirely on his own and it surprised most of his followers. He changed his mind again later, and in 1937 announced that the ALN would field candidates in the next provincial election, not realizing that for all practical purposes the death knell of the ALN had already sounded long before.

After their defeat and the consequent confusion and dissensions within the party, the Liberals held a provincial convention in

Quebec City in June, 1938, to reconcile the various groups and opinions and to draw up a dynamic program. At the instigation of the *Ligue des Droits de la Femme*, women participated for the first time in Quebec history in a party convention. Of over eight hundred delegates only forty were women but, despite their small numbers, they made their presence felt, particularly in the resolutions and education committees. In the education committee they proposed for inclusion in the Liberal program that education should be made compulsory as it was in other parts of Canada, and that textbooks should be free and uniform throughout the province. This astonished the male members of the group, who scarcely expected such enlightened opinions from these ladies. After the meeting, one of the delegates said to me, "I never thought that women were so advanced." It was easy for me to reply that they had never had a chance to display their knowledge of these subjects in public. The presence of women at this convention gave us the opportunity to show that we are often more competent than many men in matters of education, health, and the family.

Once we had been admitted to the convention, the next step was to get women's suffrage inserted in the party program. For this a proposer had to be found. I still remember the ardour with which, to the horror of some of the delegates, I expressed my firm intention of rising and making the motion myself if no one else would. My stratagem succeeded. The resolution committee supported the proposal and it was ratified by the general assembly. The presence at the convention of Ernest Lapointe, the new Minister of Justice, certainly aided our cause. The members of the House of Commons were becoming increasingly aware of how unjust and illogical was the persistent refusal by the Quebec legislators to grant us a right we had possessed in the federal field since 1918. Though I do not wish to minimize the importance of this action by the Liberals of our province, it must be remembered that being then in opposition they did not foresee actually having to accept for some time yet a measure they had always opposed. The delegates confirmed the leadership of Adélard Godbout, who had always voted against the female suffrage bill. However, after the convention he became one of our faithful allies and we owe our final victory to him.

During that same summer of 1938, Paul Gouin decided that

a convention of all the opposition groups would be held in Sorel on the 23rd and 24th of July, marking for a second time the entrance of the ALN into active politics in Quebec. It was hoped that the movement would experience a resurgence, for people were still interested in its reform program. And, in fact the ALN did for a time know a certain success. There were enthusiastic meetings, with loudspeakers outside to enable overflow crowds to hear the speeches. I can remember monster rallies at the Saint-Jacques market in Montreal. My husband and Mr. Lapointe often came down from Ottawa on Friday evenings, and after dinner, as if for dessert, they would say, "Let's go and hear what's being said at the ALN." We would sit some distance away in the car, hoping not to be recognized, for the presence of the Speaker of the Commons and the Minister of Justice would seem to give tacit encouragement to the ALN. The party ran sixty candidates in the provincial election of October 1939 but none were elected. Later Paul Gouin accepted Duplessis' offer of the position of curator of historical monuments. This man, despite his many fine attributes, did not possess the qualities necessary to make a leader. Yet his grandfather, Honoré Mercier, and his father, Sir Lomer Gouin, had both been prime ministers of Quebec.

Action libérale tried to reform the Liberal party and, when it failed, offered itself as an opposition party. Unfortunately it played into the hands of the *Union nationale*, which used it to attain power and then become a party of the extreme right. So the positive work of two or three years in the long run gave power to reactionaries. Those who criticized the leaders of the ALN for breaking with the Liberals maintained that they should have closed their eyes to the imperfections of the Taschereau government and worked with him within the party. It seems to me, however, that if you close your eyes, you are likely to bump into something and hurt yourself badly. That, moreover, is what happened: a section of the ALN went over to the *Union nationale*, thus joining the Establishment, while the Liberal party still left much to be desired. At some point one must choose between one's personal interests and the cause one is fighting for and, if need be, abandon the traditional parties. If all those men had been willing to work as a team, our necessary reforms might have come about more quickly. Far more important than the fate of any political party is united action to shake up the masses and draw them out of their apathy and ignorance. Rather than close our eyes, we should keep them wide open and walk straight ahead, indifferent to what might happen to ourselves. Politics must aim at the ideal of the greatest common good. However, it now tries only for what seems possible, to excuse the actions of certain politicans.

VIII

Full-Fledged Citizen

Meanwhile, through political, economic, and social upheavals, the long struggle to obtain the provincial vote had continued. In 1935 our bill was sponsored by Fred Monk, an *Action libérale* member who, along with his whole party, supported the cause of women's suffrage. Regrettably, Edgar Rochette, who had once so eloquently sponsored our bill, had become the Minister of Labour in the Taschereau government and was now our most violent opponent. For, sensing how much ground the women were gaining, Taschereau had decided to put the bill this time to a party vote. It was sad to see men who had previously spoken in our favour rising to vote against a measure they had once supported. Peter Bercovitch, the member for Saint-Louis and an eminent attorney, meeting me in the corridor of the Legislative Assembly, told me with great bitterness that he was going to be forced to do a deplorable thing. Since I knew that he was an honest and trustworthy man, I did not immediately understand. Indeed how could I have imagined that he would sacrifice his principles to the extent of yielding to party discipline quite contrary to what he believed in? One Liberal minister, Honoré Mercier, though unwilling to defy his leader, preferred to withdraw rather than vote against a measure he had always supported. In this way the Monk bill was defeated by nineteen votes.

When the *Union nationale* came to power in 1936, the new Prime Minister, Maurice Duplessis, called an emergency session of the Legislative Assembly for the 7th of October. A revision of the Election Act was on the agenda, but among the amendments suggested there was no mention of women's suffrage. A delegation of women went to the Committee of Public Bills to propose an amendment to Section 12 of the bill which, by the simple elimination of the word *male*, would have put both sexes on an equal footing in matters of suffrage. Two members of the party in power, Dr. Camille Pouliot and Mr. Frank Pouliot, supported this proposal. As might have been expected, Duplessis opposed it violently and the amendment was defeated. The M.L.A.s treated the matter lightly, convinced that not much importance would be attached to a question they considered secondary; besides, they were not very much concerned about still distant elections.

I often had occasion to meet Maurice Duplessis, both before and after he gained power. He was always very pleasant and one day confessed quite frankly, "I sat opposite Taschereau for ten years. I learned his methods; in fact, I've even improved on them." And on another occasion, showing me a present he had received, "I got this from one of my ministers; he calls me 'le boss'." He was a generous man, and had the gift of speaking to humble people and making them believe that he was defending them against the encroachment of the federal government. He was paternalistic by nature and practised patronage to an incredible degree. To his way of thinking everything could be bought – the opinion and support of anyone at all – and he shamelessly courted the financiers, the *curés*, the English, etc. While in the Opposition, he used to annoy Taschereau by proposing minor amendments to our bill, thus giving us a bit of hope, but always voted against the principle. The opinion of others was the least of his concerns and if anyone dared to accuse him of arrogance, he simply shrugged and replied, "So what?" One day, I heard him introduce a well-known speaker from France, beginning with these words: "We here are improved Frenchmen." Mute with astonishment and shock, the audience could only wonder at the boorishness and ill manners of the Prime Minister.

The reverses we suffered while Duplessis was in power stimulated the ardour of the members of the *Ligue des Droits de la Femme*. We resolved to obtain greater co-operation from the various women's organizations in Montreal and Quebec City and also from rural women. We therefore launched a drive to raise about twenty thousand dollars to pay for a publicity campaign. Our efforts were crowned with success and, in newspapers and magazines and on the radio, the question of female suffrage was placed more and more before the public.

During an exhibition organized by the Canadian Manufacturers Association, a booth was put at our disposal where visitors could mark on a ballot whether they were for or against women's suffrage. The result was sensational. The Mayor of Montreal, Mr. Adhémar Raynault, chaired the meeting at which the vote was counted; it showed 8,149 people in favour of the measure and only 294 against. This indicated that the population in general was becoming increasingly favourable to us.

The depression of the 1930s had catastrophic effects upon the economic life of the country. Unemployment reached record figures; the provinces and municipalities, which were responsible for social measures, were almost paralysed by the lack of sufficient revenues to meet the needs of the people. The federal government had to contribute very considerable sums to the provinces and municipalities to provide for the most elementary requirements and even to keep some of the provinces financially afloat.

In 1934 and 1935 the Bennett government passed a number of laws authorizing the federal government to intervene in the field of social welfare—in particular to set up an unemployment insurance scheme. These laws were declared *ultra vires* by the courts, that is, not within the jurisdiction of the federal Parliament. On their return to power in 1935, the Liberals, still under the leadership of Mackenzie King, decided to hold an inquiry into the whole question of federal and provincial jurisdiction and tax-sharing, to put the three levels of government in a better position to cope with the grave and unprecedented problems of the depression. In August 1937 the federal government appointed the Royal Commission on Dominion-Provincial Relations better known to the public by the names of its two chairmen as the Rowell-Sirois Commission.

The *Ligue des Droits de la Femme* asked Miss Elizabeth Monk, an eminent attorney, to prepare a brief for submission to the commission. Miss Saint-Jean also presented a brief on behalf of the *Alliance pour le vote des femmes*. In our submission, Miss Monk briefly outlined the intolerable conditions in Quebec and set down the economic repercussions stemming from the fact that women could not vote provincially and thus were unable to give effective expression to their disapproval of certain laws that were unjust to them. She showed that the funds provided to the provinces by the federal government were not distributed equally between the sexes. For instance, of $220,000 granted to Quebec to provide technical training for young people, only $25,000–to qualify girls for domestic service–was devoted to the needs of women. Ontario, on the other hand, spent twice this sum for the same purpose.

Miss Monk maintained that the government had no right to use money that had been paid into the treasury as taxes to subsidize provincial services without specific guarantee that, in the distribution of these grants, no citizen, male or female, would be discriminated against. She drew the attention of the commission to the inanity of our provincial labour laws, which permitted one wage-scale for men and another for women in the same occupation, a discrimination that extended even to teaching. This disparity helped lower the wages paid to men, with consequent damage to the standard of living in the province and, indirectly, in the whole country. The Turgeon Report on the Textile Industry, tabled in 1936, had reached the same conclusions.

Miss Monk's statements on the low standard of living in Quebec were based on clear statistical evidence that inadequate working-class housing and malnutrition contributed greatly to the high infant-mortality rate. In eight Canadian municipalities infant mortality was more than one hundred per thousand births; all of these municipalities were in the province of Quebec. These irrefutable facts should have given pause to advocates of "the revenge of the cradle," who believed it advantageous for Quebeckers to maintain their high birth-rate. What a waste of human life, what lost energy, because our Quebec legislators were not in the least concerned with social problems. The feminists believed that granting the provincial vote to women would improve this situation.

Our brief also pointed out that the exclusion of Quebec women from provincial posts prevented their appointment to federal posts–to the Senate, for instance, or to government commissions or the judiciary. As a remedy for this, we suggested that the BNA Act be amended by the insertion of a statement condemning all discrimination based on sex or race. A similar measure was already in force in England as well as in the provinces of Alberta and British Columbia. The *Ligue des Droits de la Femme* believed that such legislation would diminish the civil and political incapacity of women in Quebec and remove the last vestiges of certain legal disadvantages still surviving on the statutes of other provinces in Canada.

The publication of our brief brought no immediate success, but it did help draw the attention of the federal government to a number of urgent problems. And as the text was distributed on request to all parts of the country, we felt that our opinions were becoming more and more widely known. But this problem had to be attacked at the source, and in 1938 we returned for the twelfth time to present our bill in the Legislative Assembly, sponsored this time by a member on the government side. It was condemned in advance for Duplessis was no trifler in matters of party discipline. Our sponsors of former years, William Tremblay and Martin Fisher, rose to vote against us. Even though ministers, they did not have the right to express a personal opinion on any subject, especially female emancipation to which their "boss" was vehemently opposed.

With a stubborness that many might find surprising, we returned to the attack early in 1938. The introduction of the bill by P.-A. Lafleur, *Union nationale* member for Verdun, provided an opportunity for the Honourable Médéric Martin to remark rather ungraciously, "The same old faces turn up year after year," and for another MLA to add that the ladies always managed to arrive with Lent to make them (the members) do penance. To our surprise the measure was adopted on first reading and sent to the Committee on Public Bills. The sole purpose of this concession – for the Prime Minister himself chaired this committee and dominated it as completely as he did the Legislative Assembly – was deliberately to obscure the issue. We had the chance to express our point of view but with no promise of action.

On the 29th of March, a small but representative delegation appeared before the committee. It included Miss Saint-Jean, president of the *Alliance pour le vote des femmes du Québec*, Miss Marguerite Wherry, president of the Business and Professional Women's Club, Mrs. John Scott of the Montreal Women's Club, Miss Irène Joly, president of the *Association des femmes propriétaires*, Mrs. Henri Vautelet, Mrs. Paul Martel and myself, members of the *Ligue des Droits de la Femme*. The ardent feminist, Mrs. John Scott, now eighty-four years old, charmed her listeners by addressing them in French. The women defended their case so skilfully that the Honourable T.J. Conan, a minister in the Duplessis cabinet, and T.-D. Bouchard, a member of the Opposition, openly declared themselves converts to our cause. Prime Minister Duplessis himself deigned to congratulate the delegation. Nevertheless, the committee rejected our request the next day and the bill was beaten on division.

In the autumn of 1939, Duplessis called a surprise general election. The women immediately launched a new publicity campaign on the radio, in the press, and in letters to the candidates. The *Ligue des Droits de la Femme* and the *Alliance pour le vote des femmes du Québec* resolutely supported the Liberal party, which had placed women's suffrage on its program. The result of the election was a spectacular defeat of the *Union nationale* and the return of the Liberals to power. But inasmuch as the new Prime Minister, Adélard Godbout, did not declare his intentions about women's suffrage in the weeks immediately following his election, I advised all interested women as a matter of prudence to remind him of his promise at the 1938 convention. Letters, telegrams, and petitions poured in from all corners of the province. The forty women delegates to the convention, all ardent Liberals needless to say, gathered hundreds of signatures for a petition that must have impressed Mr. Godbout. And on the memorable day of the 20th of February, 1940, the women's suffrage bill was included in the Speech from the Throne.

We had won the first game in the rubber, but we still had to overcome difficulties of another sort. The anti-suffragettes, both men and women, who were particularly numerous in the rural areas and had been content till then to express their opinions moderately, suddenly realized that we had government support and redoubled the violence of their attacks. Right from the beginning they had been supported by our clergy. The article by Mrs. A. Croff maintaining that the women of Quebec did not want the right to vote, which I mentioned earlier, was only one sign of an organized campaign to prevent the adoption of the measure. This was all the more shocking since a report on the attitude of the Catholic Church, published by the League of Nations in 1938, expressed a totally different opinion from that of the Quebec clergy on this point. I had suggested to the *Ligue des Droits de la Femme*, of which I was still president, that we send a copy of this report to all the *curés*; purely budgetary reasons prevented our putting this plan into action and so we lost an excellent opportunity to instruct a clergy that too often remained unaware of the more liberal attitudes of the Church.

On the 7th of March, sixteen days after the Throne Speech, there was great excitement throughout the province. An official communiqué from the highest ecclesiastical authority, His Eminence Rodrigue Cardinal Villeneuve, was published in *La Semaine religieuse* of Quebec. This important document read as follows:

> In response to numerous entreaties and to put an end to the variety of opinions ascribed to Us on the matter of the proposed bill to grant women the right to vote in provincial elections, We believe it is Our duty to declare Our feelings.
>
> We are not in favour of female political suffrage:
>
> 1. Because it is contrary to the unity and authority structure of the family;
>
> 2. Because it exposes women to all the passions and intrigues of electoralism;
>
> 3. Because, in truth, it appears to Us that the very large majority of the women of the province do not want it;
>
> 4. Because the social, economic, hygienic, and other reforms that are brought forward as recommendations for granting the suffrage to women could be just as well achieved through the influence of female organizations outside politics.
>
> We believe that We are here expressing the common sentiments of the Bishops of the province.

In the days that followed this statement, Prime Minister Godbout was silent, but I knew that he was stunned. I had an interview with him at the Windsor Hotel in Montreal during this period and I was able to realize how deeply, as a practising Catholic, he regretted that such an attitude could be held by some of our religious authorities. Under the circumstances he thought seriously of resigning as prime minister. I hastened to dissuade him from this, pointing out that if he yielded to such unwarranted pressure he would be providing grist for the mill of those who considered Quebec "a priest-ridden province." Jean-Louis Gagnon, then a young reporter in the press gallery of the Legislative Assembly, recalls what happened in Quebec City during this period. It seems that Mr. Godbout, disturbed by the campaign that was raging in the press against women's suffrage, decided to telephone Cardinal Villeneuve. He was informed that His Eminence was not immediately available. Several hours later he received a call from the Cardinal and informed him that as a submissive son of the Church, he had no intention of remaining at his post if this obstruction of the vote for women, which was being directed, unfortunately, by Catholic elements, did not cease. He would resign and ask the Lieutenant-Governor-in-Council to call the Honourable T.-D. Bouchard to form a new government. Mr. Bouchard's rather anti-clerical views were very well known. The Cardinal listened to Mr. Godbout and thanked him for his call. The next day, as if by magic, the violent objections to the bill disappeared from the pages of our newspapers. This account completely corroborates what Mr. Godbout told me personally during my interview with him in Montreal.

At the beginning of the 1940 session Maurice Duplessis, now Leader of the Opposition, asked the Prime Minister pointblank, no doubt in the belief that this would embarrass him, what his intentions were in the matter of female suffrage. Godbout replied, in effect, that he did not know in what form or at what moment the bill would be introduced in the Legislative Assembly, adding that in this case, as in that of other projected legislation, he would not permit emotions that were being stirred up for petty political motives to be exploited. "It may seem strange," he said, "but there are still people who can keep their word once they've given it."[1]

A double-edged reply if you like, which was admired by all supporters of women's suffrage and, it goes without saying, by the English press. In the French-language newspapers, however, other views could be read. Le Droit of Ottawa, which was owned by the Oblates, contended that it was "often better to go back on one's word than to continue on the wrong road." Le Devoir was inundated with vitriolic letters from various women's groups and individuals.

These letters so resembled one another that one could believe they had all emanated from the same source and the same narrow mind.

Adélard Godbout resisted these last-minute attacks, convinced he was acting justly and according to the dictates of his conscience. On the 9th of April, 1941, he introduced in the Legislative Assembly Bill No. 18, granting to the women of Quebec the right to vote in provincial elections and also to stand for election. It involved making a few amendments to the Election Act of 1936–a simple matter in parliamentary terms, perhaps, but how heavy in its consequences. It marked the crowning of incessant effort and the dawning of a new era for the women of Quebec. A good many of us, deeply moved and enthusiastic, took our places in the galleries, which had been reserved that day for women. Dr. Paquette, a former minister in the Duplessis government, and Duplessis himself, made much of the change in the attitude of Godbout, who had been one of the opponents of the measure in the past. To their criticism the Prime Minister replied, "Circumstances have changed so much in Quebec in recent years that the problem now presents itself in an entirely different light."[2] On the 18th of April, after considerable debate, the bill was adopted on third reading by a vote of sixty-seven to nine. It then had to be submitted to the Upper House where it was introduced on the afternoon of the 25th of April by the Honourable Philippe Brais. Certain hardened adversaries of women's suffrage, such as Sir Thomas Chapais and the Honourable Médéric Martin, took this occasion to speak for one last time against the measure. Nevertheless, it was adopted on third reading by a vote of thirty to five.

Through a courteous gesture of the leaders of the Liberal party, it had been arranged that the one last formality, that of royal assent by the Lieutenant Governor, should take place immediately. Thus at about six o'clock in the evening of the 25th of April, 1940, those who had worked so hard and so long for female suffrage had the pleasure of hearing the formula, *le roi le veult*, that passed the measure into law. And so ended the struggle to permit the women of Quebec, the last in all Canada, to be electors in their province.

After this victory, however, a great deal still needed to be done

94

to ensure the rights of Quebec women. Yet once the vote had been obtained, many women withdrew from this form of political activity, imagining incorrectly that their presence was no longer necessary. The *Ligue* continued its work for several years, but gradually ceased to function. Later, to my regret, I heard a certain lady remark, "Before they ask for any more rights, women should first make use of those they have."

IX

When a Woman Marries . . . .

Besides working all these years for the rights of the women of Quebec, I had spent many very interesting days at my husband's side in Ottawa. His election as Speaker of the House of Commons in 1936, after some ten years as Liberal party whip, meant greater responsibilities for me. He was now the second citizen of Canada, after the Prime Minister, and had to move in a circle where social life was very full. For our first year in Ottawa we rented a house but the following years we stayed at the Chateau Laurier. Every Tuesday Pierre gave a luncheon for ministers, members of parliament, and others connected with the government of the country. After the 1940 election he became Secretary of State in the King government and at the end of 1941 he was appointed a judge of the Superior Court in Montreal.

Prime Minister King was a charming man, though he did not easily make friends. However, one evening when we were his guests, shortly after the death of Oscar D. Skelton, the Under-Secretary of State for External Affairs, he talked at length about his life, his mother, and Mr. Skelton. We knew that he had just lost a very dear friend and was feeling terribly alone. As a bachelor, he was free to devote himself entirely to public affairs but the relative solitude in which he lived doubtless made him experience some very difficult moments. He was very much attached to his dog, which returned his affection and always began to tremble when the valet packed his master's suitcase for a trip.

Despite the difference in our ages, Mr. King thought of Pierre and myself as friends and we were often invited to Laurier House. One evening, after dinner, when we were drinking our coffee in the library, where there was a portrait of his mother, always with fresh flowers beside it, Mr. King walked over to the piano, announcing to the guest of honour, a titled Englishman, "My dog is going to sing." Somewhat startled, I wondered what was about to happen. The other guests, who included Mr. and Mrs. Lapointe, Mr. and Mrs. Gustave Lanctot, and Mr. and Mrs. Maxime Raymond, were also bewildered. Our host then sat the dog on the pianostool with its paws on the keyboard and, standing behind it, began to sing while the dog howled in unison. On our way home, Pierre said to Mr. Lapointe, "That was frightful! You who are so close to Mr. King, couldn't you have a word with him? What will our foreign guests think?" To this, Mr. Lapointe replied wryly, "I think we'd better speak to the dog." Despite the strangeness of the scene we had just witnessed, I confess that I was glad the Prime Minister had at least this faithful companion beside him.

I kept myself as free as I could from household duties and social events so that I could listen as often as possible to the debates in the House, which have always fascinated me. At the time of the abdication of Edward VIII, Mr. King invited all the members of his party to the Chateau Laurier to hear the King's farewell address over the radio, a speech we all listened to with deep emotion.

In 1937, my eldest daughter Hélène and I accompanied my husband to London for the coronation of George VI. We had the impression that the British government wished to offer the warmest possible welcome to the overseas visitors, on whom the safety of the Empire depended, for social functions followed one after the other – receptions by members of the royal family and of the nobility, by members of parliament, the diplomatic corps, the various guilds, and many others. In his capacity as Speaker of the House of Commons and in the name of all the countries of British allegiance, of which Canada was the oldest, Pierre spoke at Westminster before Parliament and in the presence of the new monarch. Mrs. Fitzroy, the wife of the Speaker of the British House of Commons, had invited Lady Hailsham, the wife of the Speaker of the House of Lords, and myself to luncheon in the Speaker's apartments on the banks of the Thames. After a delightful meal she took us into the hall where all the members of the British

Parliament and the Commonwealth delegates were gathered around their sovereign. That evening with the other delegates we had the honour to be presented to Their Majesties and entertained at dinner in Buckingham Palace. The two great banquet halls were a splendid sight; in the one where my daughter and I sat, which was presided over by the Queen, silver dishes sparkled amid bowls of flowers in delicate shades; in the other, that of the King, at whose table my husband was seated, scarlet roses set off a massive gold service.

The Coronation festivities also included a visit to Spitshead on the English Channel, where the British fleet lay at anchor. An imposing number of ships from various countries stood on guard in the harbour and we felt a sense of anguish at the sight of all those cruisers and battleships loaded with men ready for combat. England wished to show us her might and the protection we would receive in case of war. History, unfortunately, proved the contrary. Our stay in Great Britain concluded, for several of us, with a trip through Scotland.

Before our return to Canada, our delegation was invited to Paris where France held an official reception for all the Commonwealth dignitaries. There was even a large dinner reception at the Ritz Carlton Hotel under the auspices of the government of Léon Blum. Invitations had been sent out a fortnight in advance but in the interval a new government had been formed which assumed the duty of receiving us. We were struck by the contrast between a rather tranquil England and a France shaken by a series of short-lived cabinets and a great many strikes. After we had spent some time in Paris, my husband had to return to Canada but my daughter Hélène and I continued our travels on the continent. Italy especially charmed us.

On the 10th of September, 1939, the day the Canadian Parliament officially declared war on Germany and her allies, I was in the Speaker's gallery, close to Camilien Houde and Canon Lionel Groulx. Earlier that day, aware of the profound convictions of Mr. J. S. Woodsworth, the leader of the CCF and member for Winnipeg North Centre, Prime Minister King had said of him: "There are few men in this parliament for whom, in some particulars, I have more admiration than the leader of the Cooperative Commonwealth Federation. I admire him, in my heart, because time and again he has had the courage to say what lay on his conscience regardless of what the world might think of him. A man of that calibre is an ornament to any parliament."[1]

Before the vote, Mr. Woodsworth expressed his opposition to all war before a hushed and respectful House of Commons. I shall never forget how moved I was while listening to this man with the noble countenance who did not hesitate to state his convictions, even though he already knew that no member of his party would follow him. Mr. Woodsworth was not only a remarkable man but a first-rate politician. I had often seen him talking to that other great Canadian, Henri Bourassa, as they walked together in the evening on Parliament Hill. I used to think, and still do, that if they had worked together, those two men could have built a truly strong Canada. And shortly before his death–confirming what I had always thought of him–Bourassa said in a speech, "You should vote for a CCF candidate rather than for a red Liberal sheep or a blue Conservative sheep."[2]

In the hall at Woodsworth House in Ottawa, there is a letter dated 1926 and signed by Prime Minister King. It seems that in an attempt to give more stability to his minority government of the time, King had offered Woodsworth the portfolio of Minister of Labour. Woodsworth refused, but offered the support of his group in Parliament if King would agree to bring in an old age pension scheme. The Prime Minister consented orally, but Mr. Woodsworth craftily confessed that he would prefer to have written confirmation. King complied and the legislation was given parliamentary approval in 1927. Ever since I first heard this anecdote, I have felt a real spiritual kinship with the founder of the CCF.

The election of March 1940 gave the Liberals under Mackenzie King the imposing majority of 178 seats out of 245. During the campaign the Honourable Ernest Lapointe and his Quebec colleagues gave firm assurance that they would never be part of the government nor would they support it if it tried to impose compulsory military overseas service, generally known as conscription. Lapointe died on the 26th of November, 1941, when all Europe except Great Britain and Sweden was under the heel of Hitler. I have always been persuaded that he saw the coming dissensions

99

in our country, for a few weeks before his death, when he was already very ill, he asked my husband, who had come to see him after a sitting of the House, whether there had been any mention of conscription. Seeing how distressed he was, Pierre felt obliged to answer in the negative. The very next day Mr. Lapointe was admitted to the Notre Dame Hospital in Montreal, where he died three weeks later.

In December 1941, Japan entered the war with her attack on Pearl Harbor and soon afterwards took Hong Kong, Malaysia, the Philippines, and Singapore. For the allies everything was going from bad to worse, and there began to be very strong pressure in Canada for conscription. In Quebec, however, opposition correspondingly increased. Early in 1942 Mackenzie King appointed Louis Saint-Laurent, a noted Quebec lawyer who had never been involved in active politics, to succeed Ernest Lapointe as Minister of Justice. Saint-Laurent, who categorically refused to speak out against conscription, was subsequently elected to Mr. Lapointe's former riding of Quebec East.

In view of the gravity of the international situation, the federal government decided to hold a referendum on the 27th of April, 1942, to ask the Canadian people whether they would consent to release the government "from any obligation arising out of any past commitments restricting the methods of raising men for military service." The cabinet ministers travelled back and forth across the country to persuade the population to vote yes, in order to give the government complete freedom of action. In our province almost the entire population was unwilling to do so. At the Westmount polling station where I voted no, the other French Canadians did likewise. In the rest of the country, however, the majority of the population yielded to the government request. Having obtained the consent of sixty-five per cent of the voters, Mackenzie King tabled in the Commons, Bill No. 80 to amend the National Resources Mobilization Act. This bill repealed the restriction limiting compulsory military service to within Canada, which left the government free to impose conscription when and if it judged this necessary. Arthur Cardin, the Minister of Public Works, opposed the bill and left the cabinet. In his letter of resignation, he maintained that the proposed amendment was in no way justified by the military situation and absolutely incompatible with previous government statements. When Mr. King introduced the bill for second reading on the 10th of June, he tried at some length to explain and justify this new attitude. He emphasized that the government must have the power to act in case of need and coined the rather clever slogan: "Conscription if necessary but not necessarily conscription." The next day, Cardin once again explained the reasons for his opposition to the measure, pointing out that the amendment would enable the government to bring in conscription without any further consultation with Parliament or people. And yet for years the Quebec federal ministers had promised that conscription would never be imposed if Quebec consented to participate voluntarily in the war.

On Christmas Day, 1941, a thousand Canadians had been captured by the Japanese at Hong Kong; in August, 1942, several thousand more were killed or taken prisoner at Dieppe. Two years later, Canadian forces took part in the Normandy landing; the end of the war was finally in sight. More and more Canadians were coming forward to enlist but the needs were even greater. After considerable hesitation and discussion, but feeling that they were forced to take this action by heavy losses overseas, the government decided to impose conscription in December, 1944. Grave and anxious moments followed, for Canadians were divided. The mayor of Montreal, Camilien Houde, a witty and dynamic man loved by Montrealers, had been interned in August 1940 for advising the public to ignore the National Registration Act. After his release in 1944, he had said irrepressibly, while chairing a banquet of the *Societé d'Étude et de Conférences*: "Here I am again, I've been away. And you know, friends, for the last few years I've had lots of time to read." Mr. Jean Drapeau, then an eager young nationalist candidate, had declared during a Montreal by-election in 1942 that French Canadians were not very interested in a war effort to save England. The *Bloc Populaire*, founded by Maxime Raymond, and the *Ligue pour la Défense du Canada,* one of whose leading spirits was André Laurendeau, also identified themselves with Quebec nationalist feelings. Quebec's reputation in Canada suffered, for many people found it difficult to understand why Quebeckers did not feel closer to France or England, and particularly why they refused to submit to the wishes of the English Canadians.

An event that deeply moved me at this time was the disgraceful and, to my mind, unjustifiable treatment of a group of our citizens. When Pearl Harbor was attacked, Canada had some twenty-four thousand inhabitants of Japanese origin, eighteen thousand of them citizens by naturalization or birth. For reasons of national security, the government decided to evacuate them from the Pacific Coast to the interior of British Columbia. To understand the sentiment of latent hostility that exploded around the Japanese, it is useful to recall the reason for their coming to this country. Around the turn of the century, industry turned to Japan as a source of cheap labour. As early as 1908, there were violent protests against this immigration. The Canadian authorities then began to impose restrictions and, in 1928, a verbal convention between Canada and Japan limited immigration to one hundred and fifty a year. Most of the Japanese had settled in British Columbia and, as many of the professions were closed to them, they were engaged chiefly in trade, farming, and fishing. Intelligent and industrious, they were known for their thrift and their honesty, but they aroused jealousy and even antagonism among the people of British Columbia, who considered them dangerous rivals. The province even passed a law denying the vote to all citizens of Asian origin unless they had served with the Canadian forces during World War 1. When they were evacuated from the Pacific coast after Pearl Harbor, they were obliged to sell their property for ridiculous prices. Restrictions were imposed on them as on no other group of enemy origin. For instance, they needed government authorization to lease property, and an order-in-council forbade them to cross provincial boundaries without a special permit. Furthermore, when Japanese Canadians tried to enlist at the beginning of the war, they were rejected because of their racial origin.

A number of Canadians, most of them members of the CCF, became deeply concerned about the unfortunate situation of these people, and, in 1943, committees were set up in Toronto, Montreal, Vancouver, Ottawa, and other cities across Canada. I thus had the opportunity to work with Frank Scott, Paul Baby, Roger Ouimet, and Professor Forest Laviolette in a group in Montreal.

When the war ended in 1945, the Canadian government thought of sending all those who had been born in Japan back to their country of origin. A long legal battle ensued and our committees across the country fought this deportation, which was all the more tragic since families were to be separated. We were ultimately successful and it was decided that only those who wished to do so need return to their native land. Today Japanese Canadians are treated like every other citizen and relations between Japan and Canada are excellent. Let us hope that there will never be another such crisis in Canada – a crisis affecting the liberty of a whole group of our people – with as little justification as in 1942.

As soon as Canada entered the war, it became apparent that prices were going to sky-rocket. So the government set up the Wartime Prices and Trade Board under the chairmanship of Donald Gordon, a man of extraordinary intelligence and capacity for work who had already made an enviable reputation in banking. Realizing that it would be almost impossible to stabilize prices without the help of the consumer, Mr. Gordon decided to appeal to Canadian women, who generally held the purse strings and thus exercised some control over the cost of living. He summoned the presidents of all the national women's organizations to Ottawa and suggested that surveillance committees be set up across the country. This was not an attempt to turn women into informers, but simply a necessary measure to ensure the economic stability of Canada. It was decided at the founding meeting that the country should be divided into thirteen districts or regions. Charlotte Whitton, who was well known through the various positions she had held in the National Social Welfare Council and the University Women's Clubs, was put in charge of six of these districts, comprising western Canada and part of Ontario. The other seven were entrusted to me, since I had the advantage of being bilingual. Within the space of a few months, women's committees were functioning across Canada. The success of the Wartime Prices and Trade Board was the envy of other nations, particularly the United States, where similar operations left much to be desired. Competent as they were, Donald Gordon and his assistants would not have been so successful without the help and support of the women of Canada. As a result it could be said that "this was proof that women were excellent citizens." It was also a very effective way to help win the war.

All across the country the members of the various women's clubs we visited helped set up local committees. Offices of the Prices Board were opened and our committees worked in co-operation with them. I myself went to Charlottetown, Halifax, Moncton, Saint John, Quebec City, and Montreal, as well as to northern Ontario, where there is a large group of French Canadians. Most of these journeys were by air. As soon as I arrived in a city, I would meet with the members of the women's organizations and various groups of important citizens. I remember being the only passenger on a flight to Charlottetown. It was bitterly cold and snow was falling in huge flakes. Alone in the cabin, cut off from the pilots, I wondered anxiously whether we would land safe and sound. When I reached my destination, I had some difficulty obtaining the little glass of brandy that saved me from a bad case of the flu. From Prince Edward Island I flew to Halifax. All the windows of the aircraft were covered with heavy curtains for it was considered dangerous in wartime to allow passengers to have a view of the port. During this period, I was involved in a curious incident in Saint John. At the end of a meeting in one of the theatres of the city, I had asked the audience to sing *O Canada*, and next morning someone from the Prices Board phoned my hotel to ask why I had chosen this anthem instead of *God Save the King*. I replied that it seemed a perfectly natural choice to me and that I had no intention of doing otherwise in the future.

Donald Gordon issued a regulation one day that in order to save cloth, trousers would no longer have cuffs. As I couldn't see the use of such a measure, I asked him what his mother would have done when he was a teenager on his way to becoming six foot four, if she hadn't been able to use those turned-up pieces at the bottom to let down his pants as he grew. When he said to me, smiling, a year later, "Madame, you were perfectly right about that ruling I made to try to save a bit of cloth," I found the simplicity of such an important man quite delightful. He later became president of the Canadian National Railway, and, in about 1951, there was a fierce controversy about the choice of Queen Elizabeth as the name for the new company hotel in Montreal.

When I happened to meet him at this time, I could not help reminding him of his mistake about "the cuffs on the pants." He assured me that he had nothing to do with the choice of name for the new hotel.

My husband was very liberal in his opinions and always encouraged my social and political activities. Every time I had to go to Quebec City he always sent me flowers or a telegram. In Ottawa, too, I was sure of his support. I accompanied him everywhere, whenever it was possible; when it was not, I always waited impatiently for him to come home and then we would exchange views at length about our various activities.

X

A Woman on the Hustings

For many years, I was involved with social problems and gradually I came to realize that, in a democracy, decisions are made ultimately in our parliaments. As I considered politics to be the art of governing with a view to the common good, I felt increasingly that if social action is to be effective, it should be directed toward politics. After women obtained the federal vote, my name was mentioned in the press as a possible candidate in the following election. The Liberals even offered me a riding–one that would be difficult to win, needless to say, and even more so by a woman. Officially the gesture had been made. As I had young children and was married to a Member of the House of Commons, this publicity was very embarrassing to my husband and myself. I had neither the time nor the inclination to run for parliament and my home was of first importance to me.

When Pierre was appointed to the bench in 1942, the picture had changed. My children were grown up and I realized that for French-Canadian women the rather remote and uninvolved role of lady patroness no longer fitted the context of the times. In most circles it was believed that a woman should confine herself to keeping house, bringing up her children and, above all, never expressing an opinion in public that was contrary to her husband's. In March, 1942, I had a foretaste of the sort of reaction any increase in my activities outside the home would bring when I said in a speech to the *Société d'Étude et de Conférences*, "We will emerge from our struggle weakened if we remain turned in upon ourselves with no other horizons but those we have always known and if, led by false teachers, we remain attached to the old traditions alone." The editor of *Le Bien Public*, in Trois-Rivières, picked up my remarks in his issue of the 26th of March and suggested that I return forthwith to my pots and pans: "Let her cook, sew, embroider, read, card wool, play bridge–anything rather than persist in her dangerous role of issuer of directives." My entry into active politics would clearly arouse a host of prejudices and make many people criticize me. The case was even more delicate for the wife of a judge. In any event, with Pierre's consent, I decided to participate more directly in the political life of my country and stood as an Independent Liberal candidate in a by-election held in November, 1942, in Charlevoix-Saguenay, the riding my father, a Conservative, and my husband, a Liberal, had represented successively for more than forty years.

My opponents had one thing in common: they were determined at all costs not to permit a woman candidate to triumph. They were four: Frédéric Dorion, today Chief Justice of the Superior Court of Quebec, the Conservative candidate; Émile Gaudreault, a lawyer in La Malbaie, and Émile Boivin of Baie-Saint-Paul, both former organizers for my husband, and a Mr. Lacroix, these last three all Independent Liberals like myself. So as not to displease the Ottawa Liberals, Prime Minister Godbout did not choose to give public support to any Liberal candidate.

My campaign was long and difficult. I had to cover a riding that was at least seven hundred miles long, stretching from Château-Richer near Quebec City to Blanc Sablon, not far from the coast of Newfoundland. I used car, truck, snowmobile, train, ship and canoe and I often had to travel for more than a day at a time under very difficult circumstances to reach Anticosti Island, which was also part of my territory. This hunting and fishing domain of Senator Meunier of France always reminded me of his famous *Chocolat Meunier*, a favourite treat when I was a child. I travelled along the north shore of the St. Lawrence in a ship of the Clark Line, stopping at places along the coast: Baie Comeau, Sept-Îles, Havre-Saint-Pierre, Goose Bay, Mutton Bay, and Natashquan. (At the last-named I was told that, before the war, a German freighter had spent several weeks moored at the dock. Her crew had made contact with the inhabitants and had left clothing and other articles that they promised to return for the next year. The people of the village wondered whether these sailors had been sent to study the topography of the coast, which was quite plausible since German submarines had penetrated the Gulf and managed to sink several ships.) My fellow-passengers were people of every age and from every walk of life: commercial travellers, lumberjacks, mothers with babies, nuns. In the stern a great many hens cackled happily in their cages. My husband had not wanted me to travel alone and so I was accompanied by my younger son, Paul, then aged eighteen. Our cabin looked out onto the deck and the barrels of oil under our porthole made us feel that we were quite likely to be blown to pieces at any moment. Since German submarines were prowling the river, our ship travelled at night showing no light and with noise kept to a minimum. Even the radio was silent so that the passengers' sole amusement was playing cards for penny stakes.

Pasture land was almost non-existent on that rocky coast and the people had only canned milk for their children. Few could afford this, however, and the fishermen's wives gave their babies tea; the sight of these pale, undernourished little ones distressed the mother in me. The wretched conditions in which these people lived, which were aggravated by the war, made me even more anxious to improve the lot of my compatriots. Despite all the difficulties of the journey, I found the energy necessary to carry on. At Mutton Bay we were told that a seven-year-old child had recently been devoured by huskies, which are ferocious when hungry. On this occasion, I confess, my courage failed and I did not leave the ship, contenting myself with receiving the local people on board. My son went ashore for a bit of relaxation and I did not feel comfortable till he returned. At Natashquan, the Indians, attired in their most handsome outfits, came out to meet us in canoes. For them the arrival of the ship was an important event, especially with the approach of winter when communications would be almost impossible. They took this opportunity to sell their furs, woven straw baskets, and beaded mocassins as well as to obtain provisions for the long winter months ahead.

At Clark City and Baie Comeau, I met with the notables of the town and held a number of meetings. I was then driven to a lumber-camp in Ruisseau-Vert. After sharing the hearty meal of pea soup, stewed pig's feet, and pancakes, I was handed up onto a table to speak to the men. In these somewhat rough surroundings, where a woman candidate was an object of curiosity, I encountered courtesy, even from those who did not share my opinions. I then continued to Tadoussac by car. On the way I had supper at the Bersimis Indian reserve with Dr. Barrolet, an old school friend of my husband's. At about eleven that evening, two Indians came to take me across the Bersimis River by canoe. I shall never forget that silent nocturnal paddle under the brilliant moonlight which fell in a luminous slash across the water. I then proceeded to Portneuf by truck, the only means of transport possible since the highway was under construction. Reaching my destination at about four in the morning, I met several people who were waiting for me, then went on by car to Tadoussac where, after a good cup of coffee, I consulted with my organizers. It was icy cold as I crossed the Saguenay River in a motorboat that was tossed about violently by the waves and the wind. Luckily I am a good sailor. When we landed at Baie-Sainte-Catherine the ground was covered with snow and the trip to La Malbaie was by snowmobile, which caused me some apprehension, especially on the numerous steep hills. At La Malbaie, I settled a number of electoral problems, with scarcely time to draw a breath, then went on to the last parish in my riding, arriving just in time for a scheduled meeting. After delivering my speech, I drove on to nearby Quebec City. In less than forty hours I had completed a journey of over four hundred miles and made a number of speeches without sleeping more than two hours. After this feat, I fell into bed and slept for twelve solid hours.

I believe I was the only one of the five candidates who covered the entire riding. The presence of German submarines in the Gulf may have frightened some of them. Unfortunately the results did not correspond to my efforts and I came second in the race; Frédéric Dorion was the victor. The outcome of my first election campaign left me with feelings of both satisfaction and disappointment. I was happy to have shown what a woman could accomplish and had given my four male opponents a close race. What pained me most was not being elected in Charlevoix, where I had spent all my vacations since my youth and had deep ties and knew a great many people. It would have pleased me to be their representative in the House of Commons where no French-speaking Canadian woman had ever sat; I would have endeavoured, like my father and my husband, to serve their interests and those of my fellow-countrymen in a positive fashion.

During the campaign, I received several proofs of affection that touched me deeply. For instance, Mr. Lorenzo Gauthier, a well known Montreal businessman, phoned me one day at La Malbaie. "Madame," he said, "I owe my education to your father. I am successful today, but I've never had a chance to show my gratitude to your family. When your husband was Speaker of the Commons and minister, you didn't need anyone; today you're almost alone and forsaken and I'd like to help you." He was as good as his word and went to his native village in Charlevoix where he worked for me for a fortnight without pay. His efforts were crowned with success and I obtained an imposing majority in that place.

And again, a Montrealer, today a judge, went to a remote La Malbaie concession one evening to speak on my behalf to an audience of about two hundred people. "Ah, madame," he told me, "if only you could have heard me! I spoke so well that I made them cry." In this case, I've always felt that he might have done better to make them laugh, for on polling day, out of two hundred ballots cast, only two were for me. I was more appreciative of the comment of a doctor of La Malbaie after the campaign: "If I'd known you better in time, I would certainly have worked and voted for you." This from a good Conservative was a consoling remark and compensated slightly for the support that a prominent Liberal gave to the Conservative candidate. I am speaking of Jean-François Pouliot, the member for Montmorency, who is supposed to have said in a speech: "If Mme. Casgrain is elected, all you'll need to do when you want to obtain favours from the Liberal party is ask her to go and have tea with Mr. King." He wished to imply that Mr. King would be susceptible to feminine charms and that social life should be enough for any woman. Mr. Pouliot had probably never forgiven my husband, impartial in his capacity as Speaker, for expelling him from the House for a flippant remark about the Leader of the Opposition, Mr. Bennett–a remark he had refused to retract. At this period, some professed Liberals were really conservative in spirit and Jean-François Pouliot acted as Frédéric Dorion's sponsor when the latter took his seat in the House. Mr. Pouliot had close ties with Duplessis and agreed to his demand to have our parish code revised.

In my election platform, I spoke out openly against conscription. The Liberals had opposed this measure in all their election campaigns of the previous twenty-five years and had condemned the Conservative Mr. Borden for bringing in conscription against the wishes of the French Canadians during World War I. And now these self-same Liberals were trying to get the measure accepted by our people, on the insistence of their leader, Mr. King, and others of his cabinet. After all that had been said on this matter, it is easy to understand the resistance of the population. This attitude among French Canadians could also be explained in another way; in the army, English was used almost exclusively and when a recruit came from a remote village, unable to speak the language, it was very difficult for him. Few English Canadians understood all the implications of this problem. I once heard a member say in the House of Commons, "Why should French Canadians become officers of high rank, we can't trust them. One must not forget they have been conquered."

But though I opposed compulsory service overseas, I believed in the need to help Canada and urged all the people of my riding to do their duty and respond voluntarily to the call of their country. I also opposed what were known at that time as "cash grants" to England: that is to say, funds lent to the Churchill government for war purposes. A large proportion of the English-speaking public censured me and few French Canadians were prepared to defend me. According to my critics, I was wrong to be an Independent Liberal and should, as was customary, have adhered to one of the two old parties and accepted its demands. A great Canadian, however, came to my assistance. This was Frank Scott, a McGill professor and founding member of the CCF, who wrote an open letter to the Montreal *Gazette* in which he said that no one had the right to insult me for expressing my feelings candidly and that my opposition to conscription certainly did not mean that I was an enemy of my country. However, many of the electors of Charlevoix, who had formerly called themselves friends, lacked the courage to support me and abandoned me completely.

I very quickly realized that the leaders of the Liberal party, both federal and provincial, did not want me as a member. Not only was I a woman, but they knew that if I were elected they would not be able to make me accept ideas I had already rejected. Also, I would not have changed my opinion simply to follow the leader of my party. There may also have been some fear of the possible repercussions from the election of the first Quebec woman to the federal parliament. In short, they supported no one during the campaign and it became a free-for-all. Once the election battle was over, my interest in social and political activities continued.

After strong pressure from the CCF, the Liberal majority in parliament introduced a family allowance plan. This proposed legislation was violently fought by the Conservative opposition, which saw it as a way of buying the votes of Quebeckers who had large families. Miss Charlotte Whitton, an ardent worker for that party, even published a pamphlet opposing the bill, which she termed "baby bonus for the province of Quebec." George Drew, then Prime Minister of Ontario, expressed a similar opinion on the radio.

The measure came into force in July, 1945, providing a monthly payment of five to eight dollars according to the age of the child. The federal Minister of Health and Welfare was authorized to determine the methods of applying the act and designate which of the parents should receive the allowance. In the case of orphans or wards, a third party could be designated. In view of the particular circumstances in Quebec, the French Canadians responsible for the legislation had a clause inserted making it possible – either across the country or in a particular province or category of cases – to prevent paying the allowance to the parent designated by the regulations. The Deputy Minister of Health and Welfare chose the mother as the parent to whom the allowance should be paid, considering quite rightly that she would be the most likely to use intelligently and for the benefit of the family this addition to the often inadequate wages of the husband. Maurice Duplessis, who was once more Prime Minister of Quebec and jealous of provincial autonomy, did not look kindly on the federal government's becoming the benefactor of large families. A notorious anti-feminist to boot, he opposed the method of payment. As the autocrat he was, he contrived, with the help of some French speaking cabinet ministers and members of the clergy, to arrange that, in Quebec, family allowances should be paid to the fathers. The reason given was that under the provisions of the Civil Code then in force in Quebec, the husband was head of the family and its administrator while the married woman was a minor under the law.

In the spring of 1945 I happened to be in Ottawa to attend a meeting that concluded with a dinner. As I was leaving the hall, I encountered Dr. George Davidson. "Madame," he said, "there's something very serious in the wind against the women of your province." He could not say any more. Immediately the idea of family allowances came to my mind and the very next day I made an appointment with Mr. Louis Saint-Laurent, the Minister of Justice, to tell him of my fears. He confirmed them, offering the argument that, according to the Quebec Civil Code, married women were minors in the eyes of the law; so the allowance had to be paid to the fathers. This reply shocked me deeply. Though I was not a lawyer, I knew perfectly well that by tacit agreement it was generally the wife who handled the family budget. I persisted, wanting to know what civil or religious leaders had been working on the federal government against the women of my province. Surprised at my aggressiveness, he denied that there were any, but when I added that this would demean the mothers of Quebec in the eyes of all Canada by letting it be seen that they were legally incapable, he acknowledged that I was right and suggested I take the necessary steps. He on his side promised to speak to those concerned. As I left him, I added that once again we were being forced to put up a vigorous fight with the weak means at our disposal to obtain something that was so easily given to the women of other provinces.

On my return to Montreal, I immediately formed a committee with Mrs. Constance Garneau, Mrs. Laure Hurteau, Mrs. Laurette Auger, who wrote under the pen name of Jean Desprez, and several others. Many men also proved sympathetic to our cause and within a few days work was under way. Since the time at our disposal was very limited, we had to organize a vigorous publicity campaign in the press and on radio to explain the situation and urge the mothers of families to flood the Minister of Health and Welfare with letters and telegrams of protest. Help came from the *Confédéra-*

tion des travailleurs catholiques du Canada, the *Union catholique des cultivateurs*, and the *Fédération des travailleurs du Québec*, who published an open letter in the newspapers taking a stand openly and collectively in favour of the payment of family allowances to mothers.

During this period, there was a meeting of the leaders of *Action catholique* in the basement of the Archbishop's palace in Montreal, to which I was invited. Shortly before, I met Mgr. Charbonneau, Archbishop of Montreal, who assured me that I was morally free to ask that family allowances be payable to the mothers. I begged him to accompany me, for in that basement room with its grilled windows I would feel just like Daniel in the den of lions. He answered, smiling, "Go by yourself, Madame. You'll manage perfectly." Among those present, if my memory serves, were members of *Action catholique*, Canon Albert Valois, Mgr. Irénée Lussier, Father Guillemette, o.p., Gérard Filion, Daniel Johnson, François-Albert Angers, Mrs. Pierre Dupuy, and Mrs. Barabé Langlois. Almost all of them opposed the payment of family allowances to mothers and I was asked to stop my campaign. I refused categorically, adding that my actions would open doors and windows and let light into some terribly closed circles. And if the shoe fit, they could wear it. When the vote was taken, only Father Guillemette and Mrs. Langlois, the president of the *Bureau d'assistance aux familles*, were on my side.

Upon my return home, I learned that Prime Minister King wished to speak to me on the telephone. It was to say: "I've just heard of the battle you're engaged in. I'm leaving for San Francisco in a few hours for the inaugural meeting of the United Nations. I'll settle the matter when I get home."

On the 1st of July of that year (1945), the first family allowance cheques were sent out to all the mothers of Canada except those in Quebec. The latter did not receive theirs until three weeks later, for it had probably been necessary to change all the plates which had previously been made out in the fathers' names.

XI

A Dangerous Radical

I have often been asked my reasons for leaving the Liberal party and becoming a member of the CCF. If I made this decision in 1946, it was because I had long seen how badly Canada needed a political policy centred upon the common good rather than on the promotion of personal interests.

In 1929, during a dinner, I heard a financial expert predict the stock-market crash that occurred in October of that year. The other guests, who were all younger than this wise counsellor, smiled incredulously, but a few weeks later his prediction proved correct. The shock was all the greater for me personally since my family and I lost a considerable fortune within the space of forty-eight hours. When the crisis deepened and the hideous spectre of unemployment rose up everywhere, the Canadian Prime Minister, Mackenzie King, in the face of widespread need for government help, stated in the House of Commons that he would not give anything–"not even a five cent piece"–to help any province whose policies were diametrically opposed to his own. In the autumn of 1930, his administration was defeated and the Conservatives under R.B. Bennett came to power. Despite the measures adopted by the new government, unemployment continued to rise and the general situation became more and more distressing. The return of the Liberals to power in 1935 changed conditions very little.

Towards 1936, I had occasion to visit a textile mill in Valleyfield, where there had just been a disastrous and unsuccessful strike. The workers had come out of it not only more wretchedly poor than ever but terribly embittered against the fate that tied them to this trade. I was able to observe the shocking conditions in which they worked and the low wages they received. Before my return to Montreal, I tried to get in touch with the local religious leaders but they did not see fit to receive me. I also visited the mayor, who greeted me pleasantly and even had me driven to the station by a majestic policeman – no doubt to prevent further contacts that might disturb the tranquillity of those in authority.

On my return home, I wrote an article about what I had seen, but the editor of the large Montreal newspaper to whom I submitted it hesitated to print it. "It must be one of two things," I said. "My French isn't good enough or you don't agree with my ideas." The piece was accepted on the spot. Later, reports of the Ministry of Health confirmed my allegations, mentioning the high incidence of tuberculosis among workers in the textile industry and also among those in the asbestos mines where conditions were particularly bad. In addition, the report of the Turgeon Royal Commission on Textiles, tabled in the House of Commons in 1938, indicated that the very low wages paid to textile workers in Quebec helped lower the wage scale across the whole country.

Three years after the declaration of war, the picture had altered; not only had unemployment vanished as if by a miracle but there was even a shortage of manpower. During the 1930s, anyone who maintained that Canadian national production could rise high enough to ensure employment and adequate earnings for everyone was held to be a visionary. In the face of this contrast, it is easy to understand why thousands of Canadians were asking in 1942: "If money and resources can be found to produce weapons in time of war, why is it impossible to find them in peacetime to provide houses, schools, and parks?" The CCF answer was simple: "We can do all this if we have the courage to rebuild society to serve the interests of all the people instead of the interests of a few." As well as stressing the unnaturalness of the situation – when there had to be a war to provide work for the population – the party pointed out that, despite this new economic prosperity, there were still a great many injustices and inequalities due to our still imperfect democracy and the concentration of power in a few hands. This confirmed my own experience of the previous several years and gradually I turned towards those who reasoned in this way.

Since my husband was a member of parliament, I had the opportunity to study at close hand the constructive work accomplished by a small group in the Commons. My admiration for the CCF leader, Mr. James S. Woodsworth, made it even easier for me to transfer my political allegiance. One sensed in him a deep love for his fellow men, a complete unselfishness, and a passionate desire to help those Canadians less fortunate than himself. When he was a clergyman in 1917, he spoke out openly against the war. His stand so offended the leaders of his congregation that he was forced to resign and support his large family as a dockworker in Vancouver. Elected as an Independent Labour candidate in 1921, he worked in Ottawa with the Progressive party, which had won sixty-four seats in western Canada, though keeping his freedom of action. A year later, the Progressive party collapsed and its leader, T.A. Crerar became a minister in the Liberal government of the day. Some of the Progressives, who preferred to keep their independence, united under the joint leadership of Robert Gardner and Mr. Woodsworth, the spokesmen for the farmers and the workers respectively. Among them were William Irvine of Alberta, Agnes MacPhail of Ontario, the first woman elected to the House of Commons, E.J. Garland, later Canadian ambassador to Ireland, Henry Spencer, and subsequently A.A. Heaps and Angus MacInnis, who married Grace Woodsworth. They were known in the Commons as the Ginger Group. One of Mr. Woodsworth's closest associates was Agnes MacPhail, an extremely eloquent speaker to whom all the members of the House listened religiously. Despite our different political allegiances, we shared the same interests in social problems, among others conditions in our prisons, and we were warm personal friends. One day while my husband was Speaker I went to her office on an impulse to congratulate her on a speech she had just made. To my great surprise, I saw on her wall a picture of myself that she had clipped from a newspaper. She told me of her keen interest in the struggle I was leading to obtain women's suffrage in Quebec, adding that my enthusiasm would certainly make me succeed. "I hope you will keep that enthusiasm through all the difficulties of life."

Mr. Woodsworth was always greatly concerned with the problem of relations between the various ethnic groups in Canada. His loyalty to Canadians from different parts of Europe and their closeness to him were two more reasons that led this great man, a pacifist by instinct, to oppose the declaration of war in 1939. On the 18th of March, 1940, he suffered a heart attack during a meeting of the CCF national council, and never resumed his activities. Mr. M.J. Coldwell was named acting leader of the party, which was by then established as an important political force in our country.

In 1941, while my husband was Secretary of State, I was invited to speak at the national convention of the Business and Professional Women's Club in Vancouver and took this opportunity to visit Mr. Woodsworth, who was then very ill. His daughter, Mrs. Angus MacInnis, had assured me that he would be happy to see me. However, as his blood pressure was very high, his doctor had recommended peace and tranquillity, and Grace asked me not to refer to any subject that might excite him. I had the impression that the old leader appreciated my visit. Perhaps he guessed that I would some day be one of the workers for the party he had founded.

In my study of the program of the CCF, the origins and particularly its links with Quebec, I learned that though the movement had originated in the west, several English-speaking Quebeckers, such as Frank Scott and Eugene Forsey of McGill, and David Lewis, had played an important role in its foundation. Weekly meetings were held in Montreal and here the program that was adopted by the CCF in 1933 was partly drawn up. In 1932, these Montrealers joined with some Toronto intellectuals to found the League for Social Reconstruction, of which Mr. Woodsworth was named honorary president. One evening I was invited by some members of the League to a dinner in a restaurant in old Montreal. Here we discussed the problem of unemployment and the desperate situation in our country. This meeting with men and women who were so dedicated to the welfare of their countrymen impressed me profoundly, and after I returned home I reflected for a long time over these disturbing problems.

While this vanguard was preparing for social action in the east, other groups in western Canada were planning large-scale political activity. The United Farmers of Alberta decided at their annual convention in 1932 to seek the co-operation of industrial workers. That year socialist and reform groups from all parts of the country met in Calgary; before they separated, they had founded the Co-operative Commonwealth Federation. In my research into this historic meeting, I regret that I did not find any French-Canadian names among those present. A year later, at their first convention in Regina, the CCF became a national political party and issued a manifesto in which it clearly stated its intention to replace by peaceful means "the present capitalist system with its inherent injustices and inhumanity by a social order from which the domination and exploitation of one class by another will be eliminated (and) in which economic planning will supersede unregulated private enterprise." This convention seems to have been the most representative ever held in our country; people from every walk of life played an active part in the drawing up of the program of a national political party.

The CCF had great difficulty establishing itself in the province of Quebec, in large part because of the power of the Catholic Church, even though the Church also criticized existing social structures and showed an ardent desire to remedy them. The reforms advocated by the CCF were perhaps not of Catholic inspiration, but they certainly stemmed from Christian principles. However, our religious leaders considered the party suspect and, in 1934, Mgr. Georges Gauthier, the Archbishop of Montreal, published a pastoral letter entitled, "The Social Doctrine of the Church and the CCF," in which he condemned three points in the CCF program: "The suppression or excessive diminuation of private property, the class struggle, and a materialistic concept of the social order." The letter was a warning rather than an explicit order for Catholics to disassociate themselves from the party. In 1938, Cardinal Villeneuve expressed the same views in an address to the Canadian Club of Montreal and other churchmen also criticized the CCF. In those days Catholics followed the counsels of their bishops without asking too many questions; from that time the faithful of the diocese of Montreal no longer dared support the CCF, while Catholics in the rest of Canada remained hesitant. Maurice Duplessis did not much help the cause by constantly identifying socialism with communism in his speeches and repeating to anyone who would listen, "Socialism is the vestibule of communism."

Several Quebeckers, Catholics and others, found this situation very troubling, both from the religious and from the Canadian point of view. In their opinion it was serious to see the Church condemn a political party in this way. There was danger of such a stand doing more harm than good by arousing hostility and exposing the Church to criticism and conflict. Furthermore it thus rejected any possibility of influencing CCF policies itself, thereby often producing the very results it sought to avoid. There had been a similar situation in the nineteenth century when the Church condemned economic liberalism, and the Canadian bishops attacked the Liberal party. Then, in 1877, Laurier delivered a historic address at the Canadian Club in Quebec City in which he stated that the Church was confusing a philosophy known in Europe as Liberalism and another very different philosophy of Anglo-Saxon tradition prevailing here. He managed to convince the bishops that the difficulty was chiefly one of semantics, and Rome ratified this point of view. This was a happy day for the Church and for Canada because if the Liberal party had been condemned, the action of the bishops would have, by reaction, driven people away from the Church.

In the autumn of 1942, Murray Ballantyne and some of his friends tried to persuade the bishops to regard the CCF as they did the other parties–neutral from the standpoint of faith and morals. These men were not acting from political motives but as Christians seeking the good of their Church and their country. In October 1943, after a luncheon meeting that included Mgr. Charbonneau, Frank Scott, and M.J. Coldwell, the bishops assembled in Quebec City issued a statement that, while condemning communism, advocated social and economic reforms and supported co-operatives. They specified that "in their capacity as spiritual counsellors of the Catholic population they left to the faithful all freedom to adhere to any political party, provided that this party supported the fundamental Christian principles traditional in Canada and also provided that it favoured those necessary reforms in the economic and social order that are called for with such insistency in the pontifical documents."[1] Commenting on this statement, Mr. Omer Heroux wrote in *Le Devoir*: "We do not believe we are exaggerating the significance of this statement or reading too much into the bishops' words if we conclude that after an inquiry into the social program of the CCF they do not consider it necessary to prevent the faithful from joining the party or bearing its colours in the federal as well as in the provincial field."[2]

Other analysts were less convinced, and a prompt and violent reaction followed the bishops' statement. Members of the old parties claimed that the moment had been badly chosen. Defenders of capitalism and private enterprise spoke of treason. This controversy astonished many Catholics. There were reports from Quebec City and Toronto that Cardinal Villeneuve and Archbishop McGuigan had received visits from important representatives of the political and financial world who considered the bishops' statement "a disastrous, naive, and ill-advised error," for in their opinion "it actually opened the way to revolutionary forces at a moment when the structure of free enterprise was in danger."[3]

Be that as it may, the work of the CCF was not made much easier by this controversy, and some rather extremist statements of certain party members, among others Mr. Harold Winch, the provincial leader in British Columbia, only added to these difficulties. It is probable that several members of the party feared to see a Catholic element enter the CCF and wished to prevent such an infiltration. Mr. Winch's indiscretions could not be let pass in silence by the Catholic leaders in his province. On the 1st of November, 1943, Archbishop Duke of Vancouver answered him from the pulpit of the cathedral, saying in substance that all the political parties were prepared to make reforms and that the anti-communist position of the CCF was at least worthy of approbation. It was difficult, however, to issue a statement on CCF policy since the party had not sufficiently defined its national program and permitted the provincial leaders to express divergent views.

Despite these obstacles, the CCF continued to make progress and in September, 1943, the Gallup Poll showed that it was the most popular of all the parties. This revelation was certainly not unconnected with the decision of the federal government to introduce a wide program of social security the following year. In 1943, the CCF carried thirty-four of the eighty-eight seats in the Ontario provincial elections, thus becoming the official opposition. It even won a seat in Quebec in the provincial election of 1944 in the new riding of Rouyn-Noranda.

I observed with growing interest the evolution of this reform party *par excellence* and was entirely in agreement with the social measures it had recommended in Ottawa through the years, such as unemployment insurance, old age pensions, and family allowances. One question often came to my mind: "Why do the proposals for social measures always come from the CCF and never from the Liberals?" The answer was clear. The latter, as capitalists, were not always anxious for social reform. But they were also opportunists, and, when they became conscious of popular pressure towards social legislation, they found it advantageous to adopt the CCF proposals. I also questioned myself about the nature of socialism and quickly observed that there is an important distinction between the socialism that presupposes absolute dictatorship as practised in the communist countries and democratic socialism as conceived by the Fabian Society in England. I could see this second type of socialism put into force by the Labour Party in England as well as in Sweden and Norway. It was this kind of doctrine that attracted me to the CCF, which has always maintained that "money should be used to serve man and not man to serve money."

XII

My Years in Active Politics

On the 11th of December, 1946, I officially joined the CCF party. Professor Frank Scott, the president of the national council, and Guy Désaulniers, the provincial leader, were my sponsors and signed my membership card. In my particular circle this news caused immense surprise; to act in this way, those around me believed, I must be a communist at the very least. However, before entering the ranks of the CCF, I had discussed the matter at great length with my husband, who had encouraged me with these words, "I made my career in the Liberal party but I can very well understand that you might take a different road." He thus left me free to act as I chose and always followed my activities with keen interest. For instance, while I was attending the CCF party convention in Vancouver in 1950, Mackenzie King died. Pierre sent me a telegram, asking me not to forget to have a message of condolence passed by the convention.

From 1946, then, I worked in a group whose principal object was to persuade Quebeckers of the need to adopt measures that would promote the common good. In this atmosphere, I soon felt completely at ease, especially since many of my co-workers were old acquaintances whose fathers had played important roles in the history of our country. In Quebec, for instance, there was the lawyer Jacques Casgrain, grandson of J.A. Mousseau, a former prime minister of Quebec, and brother of Perrault Casgrain[1], a minister in the Godbout government. A distant cousin of my husband's, Jacques Casgrain had come to Charlevoix while still a law student to help in an election campaign. A handsome young man, bilingual and a brilliant speaker, with a warm and friendly manner, he had been a much-appreciated addition to the CCF. The reasons for his joining the party reveal much of the atmosphere of the time.

When just starting out during the depression, he had practised in a working-class neighbourhood, living there himself with his wife in a very modest flat without bath or central heating. His professional fees amounted to fifty cents, a godsend for people taken to court for arrears in their rent or who had their hydro cut off when they were unable to pay their bills. This climate of misery had sickened the young lawyer, and turned him against a system that permitted the majority of its citizens to live in the insecurity, want, and, above all, humiliation of "direct relief." Later, when war was declared, he was struck by the fantastic efforts exerted by the various governments to build factories, find shelter for an army, control the economy, manufacture arms, and so on – an initiative very different from the inertia of peacetime, when it had seemed impossible to build decent housing or find work for the people. "Many people of my generation or younger," he told me, "drifted at that time on the edge of the CCF, casting an inquiring eye at its program but hesitating for the most part to commit themselves. This was probably because of the confusion between the CCF and communism, or even atheism or anti-clericalism. Dr. Louis-Philippe Roy, the editor-in-chief of *Action catholique*, felt a particularly ferocious hatred for the CCF. So one day I quoted to him Henri Bourassa's remark that Christ would be a revolutionary and if he returned to earth he'd be excommunicated and banished from the rectories. It used to shock me to see a paper called *Action catholique* accept even the most dubious sort of advertising. That was its right but it led one to think that there was a great gap between its principles and its conduct." It was difficult to get new ideas accepted in Quebec. Jacques Casgrain had learned this as I had, and he continued, "People were inclined to agree with us. They came to see us, read the books of Frank Scott and David Lewis, admitted that the CCF program was good, just, and practical but simply were unwilling to commit themselves. The tragedy of Quebec, which has led to the present situation, is that our élite in those days failed in their duty. Many remarkable men who in their hearts were radicals and reformers sacrificed their ideals to their careers rather than suffer the repeated defeats of a new party. Some, in a hurry to achieve positions of leadership on the political scene, preferred the well-paved avenue of the Liberal party to the rough footpaths of the CCF." I had seen many instances of this in Ottawa and Quebec City and that was why I had made the same choice as Jacques Casgrain.

There was also Jacques Perreault, a law professor at the *Université de Montréal*, and a director of *Le Devoir* which had strongly supported me in 1945 on the family allowances question. It gave me great pleasure to work with this brilliant man whose influence on his own generation was so great. He saw very clearly the problems the CCF had to face in our province, such as the difficulty of understanding social and cultural conditions and the lack of contact between the leaders of the party and various groups such as the business community, the intelligentsia, the working class, and the farm co-operatives. He believed that it was more important to attack such basic problems as education, housing, and social security rather than place too much emphasis upon federalism.

William Dodge, today secretary-treasurer of the Canadian Labour Congress and a governor of McGill, was a CCF candidate in the 1948-49 election and many times after that—in Verdun, Saint-Laurent-Saint-Georges, Compton, and several other ridings. Around 1934, Mr. Dodge and some of his co-workers had heard that a left-wing party had been founded in western Canada. Admirers of Woodsworth and his associates in the Commons, these young men followed the beginnings of the CCF with enthusiasm and formed a club to support it. This Verdun group became the nerve-centre of the intellectual left.

Among those who welcomed me into the CCF were Frank Scott and David Lewis, men for whom I already felt great admiration and respect. Their names are permanently connected as co-authors of *Make This Your Canada*. Both bilingual, they communicated easily with Quebeckers and often served as a link between our little group and the other members of the party. A professor of law at McGill and founding-member of the League for Social Reconstruction and the CCF, Frank Scott devoted himself body and soul to organizing a third political party in Canada. Everyone trusted his judgment and constantly sought his advice on abstract or practical matters. He is one of the most eminent men in our country.

Mr. David Lewis, who held the post of national secretary and lived in Ottawa, often came down to lend support to our Quebec group. As a student at McGill he had been president of the university socialist club. His academic success encouraged him to apply for a Rhodes Scholarship. One of the judges who interviewed him was Sir Edward Beatty, the chancellor of McGill and president of the Canadian Pacific Railway. Among other things, Sir Edward asked him if it was true that he was president of the McGill Socialist Club and what would he do if his party came to power. Lewis replied airily that he would immediately nationalize the CPR. This response keenly impressed Sir Edward, who saw qualities of intelligence and courage in this young man and immediately awarded him the scholarship. In 1942 Lewis was CCF candidate in the by-election in Cartier, in which the communist Fred Rose was victorious.

It was not very easy to work for a party that was under merciless attack from those in power, without election funds, and faced with an ill-informed public opinion. We were at a disadvantage on almost every front and in order to subsist we had to rely on the generosity of our friends and supporters and on small contributions, some of them from store-owners and industrialists. This money was used to pay the required two-hundred-dollar election-deposit and provide modest publicity. As the CCF refused on principle any donations it considered too high from business, we often had to club together to rent a hall for our meetings. I remember an election when, to obtain free political time on the CBC for the next four years, a party had to field at least twenty-two candidates. I had vainly insisted that we must have twenty-four candidates available in case of accident or defection. Events proved me right. On the eve of the election, we learned to our horror that one of our candidates on Montreal Island had just vanished. When our vice president, William Dodge, said it would be impossible at this late date to find another candidate on the Island, I suggested that he go and search elsewhere. Accompanied by Matthew Blackwood, a former pilot and now working for the CNR, who was already a candidate on the south shore, he set out that very evening. By midnight they had covered two ridings and were in the Eastern Townships where the farmers, although sympathetic, did not wish to enter the arena. At five the next morning Mr. Dodge phoned me from Compton: "Nominations close at two this afternoon and I still haven't found anyone." To which I replied, "Bill, run yourself," and, optimistic as always, I added, "You're sure to be elected." He immediately scoured the farms to obtain the twenty-five signatures necessary for his nomination papers and at five minutes to two that afternoon, we had our twenty-two candidates and free radio time for the next four years. Bill received eighty-five votes. Those were truly heroic times. I have always felt immense respect for those two men who, half dead with exhaustion, performed a giant's work that night. I am always delighted to see Mr. Dodge again and two years ago at a dinner that the CCF/NDP graciously gave in my honour, I was happy to renew my friendship with Mr. Blackwood, an energetic man who is devoting his leisure to the public service, notably at the credit union branch of Greenfield Park.

At a national convention held in Winnipeg in 1948, I was elected in absentia to one of the posts of vice president, a responsibility I gladly accepted, for my election showed very clearly that the CCF had no prejudice against women. On my return to Montreal, I received the following letter from Frank Scott, dated August 27, 1948:

> I think you have done a very courageous, and, if I can use the term, Canadian thing in accepting the vice-chairmanship. The CCF is too big today to be safe without influential guidance and advice from Canadians of French origin; both for the sake of the party, of the French Canadians themselves, and of Canada, as it is very important that all the great factors that exist in the country should be represented in our council. You are doing more for Canada than your friends will ever realize in your new position. . . . This is a difficult role we have chosen for ourselves but someone has to do the work, or else the social forces at work might get out of hand and destroy most of the things we value.

During the 1949 election campaign, which terminated in a Liberal victory, Mr. Saint-Laurent described the CCF as "Liberals in a hurry," to which I replied, "That's better than Liberals lagging behind." As might have been expected, my reply made little stir, whereas the words of the Prime Minister were picked up everywhere.

When I joined the party, our office was at the corner of Guy and St. Catherine Streets. Mr. Roger Provost was our secretary; an intelligent and active man, he later became president of the *Fédération des Travailleurs du Québec*. In 1949, our financial difficulties forced us to transfer our lares and penates to a little unheated store in the east end. A stove provided a semblance of warmth, but in winter we often had to keep our coats on during meetings. Most of the work was done voluntarily, which led to frequent changes of office staff. One day I offered the position of secretary to Gérard Pelletier, one of our sympathizers, then a journalist at the *Confédération des travailleurs catholiques du Canada* and today Secretary of State of Canada. He declined and suggested Reginald Boisvert, then editor of *Le Front ouvrier*. The latter accepted the position and took charge of our newspaper *Debout*. Roger Lemelin, the well-known writer, attended the CCF convention held in Montreal in .1944 and was a contributor to our paper. Later I was able, with his permission, to use one of his articles in an election campaign.

In 1950, Jacques-Y. Morin became our secretary. As an active member of the CCF youth group, he was well abreast with our work and gave himself to it without reserve; on several occasions he even sacrificed his own salary to pay the office rent. He had been strongly influenced by Robert Calder, an eminent French-speaking jurist and criminal lawyer of the Montreal Bar, who had published a pamphlet attacking the Taschereau government enti-tled *Comment s'éteint la Liberté*, which he dedicated to the popular leader of the Rebellion of 1837, Jean-Olivier Chénier of Saint-Eustache. Mr. Calder had supported socialism with his usual dynamism and fire and stood as CCF candidate during the 1939 provincial election, in which he was narrowly defeated. At his study circle, the CCF Wednesdays, which were held every week in the National Monument, he gave courses in political economy that were followed by discussions. It was rather reminiscent of the leftist workers' universities during the depression. Many who attended such classes, now in their sixties, received their political and social education in this way. Some of them, who were illiterate, learned to distinguish between anarchy, communism, social democracy, and other forms of government.

In 1949 another group of CCF-ers and sympathizers formed study groups with the same objective of educating the masses. Jean Boucher and Maurice Tremblay were our secretaries. Our study program dealt with the various social, political, and economic aspects of Quebec life as well as with such more general subjects as the functions of the state, the duties of the citizen, and the philosophy and nature of socialism.

As time went on, the Quebec government adopted an increasingly rigid attitude toward labour. In fact, on the 19th of January, 1949, it entered on the order paper in the Legislative Assembly a bill to establish a Quebec labour code. This proposed code contained the most repressive clauses: it would have interfered unreasonably in the democratic functioning of trade unions, limited their growth, and even threatened their existence. In addition it would have set state-controlled regulatory bodies over them similar to those found in totalitarian countries. After consultation, the various trade union federations – the FPT, the CTCC and the CCL – decided to oppose this legislation. A delegation of about four hundred trade unionists and sympathizers, of which I was a member, left Montreal on a special train that I had helped organize to protest at the Legislative Assembly in Quebec City. When we reached the old capital, we set out towards the legislature on foot through streets that were covered with dirty, melting snow. As I joined the parade I recalled the days when my father had organized the Quebec streetcar service known as Quebec Railways. Plodding along now through the mud, I could not help thinking that time changes all things. In the face of this general outcry, the Duplessis government decided to withdraw the bill. On our return journey, a trade unionist who had little love for the CCF but rather more for the bottle, spoke to me somewhat rudely and was smartly ticked off by another worker, "You shut up and leave the 'little mother' of Quebec alone!"

At the time of the strike in Asbestos in 1949, even though the Quebec wing of the CCF had no representatives in the provincial Assembly or the Commons, our federal members sent us a generous contribution to assist the families of the strikers at Christmas. It will be remembered that Prime Minister Duplessis never forgave the Archbishop of Montreal for also trying to help these families.

When Mgr. Charbonneau resigned in 1950 (on the pretext of his health, which had seemed excellent the previous 25th of November when he dined at our house with the Honourable Vincent Massey and members of the Massey Commission), Pierre and I sent him a letter regretting his departure, to which he replied:

> I want to thank you with all my heart for your most sensitive expression of sympathy on the occasion of my abrupt departure from Montreal. I had felt the storm approaching for some time–its violence broke my wings. Letters such as yours almost make me forget my pain.

Several months later I attended the CCF national convention in Vancouver and would have liked to visit him in Victoria where he had become "Father" Charbonneau, a hospital chaplain. But I had to content myself with a telephone call, for I had to hurry back to Montreal after the meetings to see my husband, whose health was causing me great concern.

In 1951 I was delegated, as one of the vice-presidents, to represent the CCF at a meeting of COMISCO in Frankfurt, Germany. The trip was both interesting and instructive. I travelled from Paris to Frankfurt by car and was struck by the enormous differences between France and Germany. After the rather neglected French countryside, the German villages looked neat and trim. One could sense a force and dynamism in these people that gave one cause to reflect, and I was more convinced than ever that they must never be rearmed. Along the way I visited the American headquarters in Heidelberg, where a company of black soldiers was drilling with a precision that reminded me of the dancers at Radio City, New York. I wondered what the Germans might be thinking about this. Installed in a comfortable, recently built Frankfurt hotel, I could see from my windows men, women, and children searching through great piles of rubble for bricks to build themselves temporary shelters.

Some twenty countries were represented at the COMISCO meetings and the official languages were German, French, English, and Italian. The association, which was based essentially on the European socialist movements, seemed to accept the presence of delegates from other continents with a certain condescension. However, the Scandinavian and Japanese representatives were particularly sympathetic to Canada; as for the English, I felt like one of their own. During the sessions, I tried in vain to get the name of Karl Marx removed from the statement of the principles of International Socialism, as well as a few paragraphs that I considered equally ill-chosen. It seemed to me that dogmatic formulae were becoming out-moded and that if we really wanted to have our doctrine accepted we had to present our aims in more practical terms. In other words, charming and delightful though a woman dressed in the style of 1900 may look, you can be sure, as the saying goes, "the boys won't follow her."

During the congress there was a huge rally at the *Congreshalle*, at which the heads of delegations addressed an audience of some fourteen thousand people. Giuseppe Saragat spoke in the name of the Italians, Victor Larocque in the name of the Belgians, Guy Mollet in the name of the French, and I myself in the name of the Canadians. Kurt Schumacher, the leader of the German socialist party, was last to address the assembly, which was very moved by the appearance of this former prisoner of the Nazis, who had lost an arm and a leg and had to lean on the young man who accompanied him everywhere in order to stand erect at the rostrum. His hold over his fellow Germans was incredible. It seemed evident that these people were restive under the yoke of the conqueror and would ultimately follow the one who would ensure their freedom and national unity. We all felt deeply troubled as we listened to his words, since it was obvious that the ruins of Frankfurt all around us were urging the Germans towards vengeance. To rearm this nation seemed sheer madness.

Towards the end of the congress there was a stormy session at which I felt it my duty to insist that in a council of nine one voice at least should be given to North America. The council of an *international* organization composed solely of eight Europeans and one Japanese seemed scarcely representative to me. The candidacy of Canada was then proposed, but our country was not elected that day despite the support of several delegates. A few days later, when I was in Bonn, Mr. Jean Chapdelaine of the Canadian embassy showed me a press release announcing that our country had just obtained a seat on the International Socialist Council, thanks to the arduous but effective work of the Scandinavian delegates.

When I left Frankfurt, I took the opportunity to increase my knowledge of European countries. After visiting our ambassador in Bonn, I journeyed down the Rhine where numerous old castles, silent witnesses of past glory, seemed to keep mournful watch over their vanquished country. In Holland, Mr. Pierre Dupuy, our ambassador, arranged for me to meet the Prime Minister and the Minister of Social Security, both socialists in a coalition government made up of socialists and Catholics. Through their kind offices, I visited some of the new moderately priced housing units that, since the war, had been built by the thousands in Rotterdam and Amsterdam. Of particular interest to me were those intended for old people since they had been built in the neighbourhoods where these people had always lived, so they need not be uprooted.

While I was away, my fellow-workers had elected me leader of the CCF in Quebec. My involvement in politics had thus become total, and during the following years I took part in all the federal and provincial elections. My work on the provincial level consisted in presiding over council meetings, speaking on the radio, and being actively involved in the organization of the various regions. At the national level, my functions were much the same and, as our French-speaking membership was small, I was often called upon to speak in Ontario or the Maritimes or some other part of Canada. Eight times I ran for election under the banner of my party. As a woman, and the leader of a party of the left to boot, I had no chance of success. However, I attained my goal, which was, above all, to make the CCF philosophy more widely known and to obtain publicity for the party. Obviously, my pursuit of a social ideal had made me renounce long ago the sort of advantages that a political career in the Liberal party might have offered me.

I endeavoured to draw a great many French Canadians into our ranks. For instance, Jacques-Yvan Morin, then a student at McGill and today a professor at the *Université de Montréal*, supported my candidacy when I ran in Verdun during the provincial election of 1952. One day he came to me. "Madame," he said, "you haven't many people to help you. Let me do what I can on your behalf." He is one of those who understand how important is the gift of self in trying to improve the living conditions of the Canadian people. His work involved going from door to door explaining

132

our program, distributing leaflets, and checking voters' lists; he also took part in the meetings in voters' kitchens, where we tried to answer people's questions and suggest solutions to their problems. This election strategy is used everywhere today. In the last provincial election Jacques-Yvan Morin was the *Parti québecois* candidate in Bourassa. Like me, he has remained faithful to his social and political ideal; only the methods by which it is to be attained sharply divide us.

My organizer in that campaign was Mr. Ben Levert, a native of northern Ontario and former mayor of Sturgeon Falls. A member of the CCF from its inception, he had always fought with tremendous courage to get the party's ideas accepted by his compatriots. The election had been scheduled for midsummer and one day several workers came to offer him the counterfoils they had received from the enumerators. Since they wanted to vote for me but were leaving on vacation, they imagined in all sincerity that we could use these receipts to "telegraph"[2] votes. Sick at heart, Levert had to explain the dishonesty of this practice and destroy the "passports." We were also often visited by the neighbourhood children, and one day a group of them decided to organize a campaign for my benefit. So on a fine summer afternoon a parade of youngsters between six and twelve appeared on the street, proudly and solemnly waving placards and pennants demanding my election. The local population was highly amused by this new sort of propaganda. On another occasion, as I was driving to my committee-room, I was stopped by a policeman who claimed that I had ignored a stop sign. I maintained that I had indeed stopped, though not for very long. He answered that that wasn't good enough; then, looking at me closely, he said, "But surely you're the woman who's hanging from all our telephone poles." And, with a broad smile, he let me drive on without more ado.

My efforts in that campaign brought me 2,857 votes, an encouraging sign but, alas, far from enough to win the day. Later that year, I received 1,135 votes in a by-election in Outremont-Saint-Jean, and in 1953 the electors of Jacques-Cartier-Lasalle gave me 2,879 votes. If I could have accumulated these votes, I would have had a seat somewhere! But despite these successive defeats, I felt that I was serving my party, and above all, my country.

While I was provincial leader of the CCF, my responsibilities absorbed all my energy and allowed free rein to my great preoccupation with improving social conditions. If it is true that satisfying work liberates, then I had become a truly liberated woman. The organization of the party was very democratic. Each member paid his fee and carried his membership card, which gave him the right to speak at all meetings. We studied each political event before establishing our official position and in this way our program was constantly improved. A steady flow of commentary left our offices on questions of the day, many of them very complex. As an example, in the spring of 1954, for the first time since World War II and without previous consultation with the federal government, Maurice Duplessis instituted a provincial income tax. To the argument that this would mean a double fiscal levy for the citizens of Quebec, Duplessis asserted the priority of the provinces in this field and demanded that the federal government grant them the right to impose such taxation. Our position on this question was based on several considerations: on one hand, an over-centralization of the federal system might jeopardize the position of French Canadians but, on the other, the federal government needed to have sufficient power to control the economy of the country. One of the chief concerns of the CCF was the protection of minority rights; in Quebec, this meant the rights of one of the largest minorities, French-speaking Canadians. That summer at the CCF national convention in Edmonton, at which Stanley Knowles and I were co-chairmen, the delegates unanimously adopted a resolution asserting that the provinces must have the revenues they required and that the rights of minorities duly recognized by the constitution must in no way be undermined or violated. The conflict in this case, then, was not so much between Quebec and the rest of Canada as between the citizens and those who wished to exploit them. In an article I wrote for *Le Devoir* early in August of that year, I tried to present this same point of view.

Being a member of the national council gave me an opportunity to work closely with such prominent members of the party as Tommy Douglas, then the Premier of Saskatchewan, and Donald MacDonald, the party leader in Ontario. My relations with these men were always pleasant and instructive, and I was struck by their good will towards French Canadians, for whom I had become the principal spokesman in the CCF. They understood the difficult struggle we were waging in Quebec against an exaggerated spirit of conservatism and widely held misconceptions about the sort of progressive proposals we were advancing. In a book published in Toronto in 1969,[3] Walter D. Young explains that nothing in the CCF movement was truly in harmony with the prevailing attitudes in Quebec. It was a foreign element, preaching centralism. The Catholic Church strongly opposed it and some English-speaking CCF-ers frequently showed great ignorance and prejudice on the subject of Quebec and the rights of French Canadians. During its short life in our province, the CCF, to many Quebeckers, had an English accent. It mattered little that Messrs. Lewis and Scott were perfectly bilingual; the CCF had no roots in the province and could show no reason for establishing any. The following events will prove how correct Mr. Young's analysis was.

On my return to Montreal after the convention, I once more attacked the special problems of my region: recruitment of new party members, our eternal financial worries, the need to convince the public that the CCF was not, as our opponents claimed, simply "an English importation." I must confess that this last problem was not made any easier by the behaviour of our members in other provinces. Early in 1955, Harold Winch, Erhart Regier, and Angus MacInnis, CCF M.P.'s from Vancouver, made statements in the House that could only be considered direct attacks on the French Canadians. Himself unilingual, Winch declared that French-speaking M.P.'s *should speak English if they wanted to be understood.* Since I knew that this narrow attitude was not shared by the majority of our members, and that the CCF had always shown great understanding for us, the provincial council (three of whose members had resigned as a result of these unfortunate remarks) protested vigorously to the national council. Experiences of this sort made me realize that the farther they are from Quebec and Ontario, the less informed are English Canadians about us. This observation was all the more painful since I was convinced, as I still am, that Canadians have a unique opportunity to prove that two cultures can co-exist to their mutual advantage within a single state.

Similar sentiments were expressed by Mr. Clement Attlee, the former prime minister of Great Britain, at our next convention, which was held in Montreal in August 1955. At this meeting, it was decided that a new name for the provincial party would more clearly indicate our objectives while ridding us of our then almost untranslatable title. As a result, the delegates voted to change the name of the Quebec wing to *Le Parti social démocratique du Québec*. I was re-elected leader and William Dodge became president of the council.

The 1956 national convention was held in Winnipeg shortly after the Quebec provincial election, in which I received 2,322 votes in Jacques-Cartier-Lasalle. "Many are called but few are chosen," runs the biblical text, and as usual I was not among the latter nor were any of our other candidates. This time, our delegation included a good proportion of French Canadians. Jacques Perreault addressed the plenary session and made an excellent impression; on the other hand Pierre Vadboncoeur, an equally brilliant man, withdrew into complete silence and did not even try to communicate with the English-speaking delegates. Michel Chartrand was also present, but, though his chatter amused everyone, his behaviour and wild statements were already beginning to arouse anxiety.

The other delegates were delighted to see this increase in the number of Quebec supporters even though we had not yet achieved any electoral success. Among the recommendations adopted at the convention was that a Bill of Rights be drawn up guaranteeing freedom of speech, the legal right to organize, equal treatment for all before the law, freedom of religion and freedom from discrimination based on sex, religion, colour, or language. Besides reaffirming its full support for the United Nations, the party stressed the urgent need to build a peaceful world and grant generous aid to the Third World. It expressed its confidence in the Canadian population, which was composed of people who had come from all the continents seeking freedom, security, and a better life. The party enthusiastically accepted the French name: *Le Parti social démocratique du Québec*, and also expressed its conviction that the Canadian federal system could assure the well-being of the nation while, at the same time, guaranteeing respect for the traditions and constitutional rights of the provinces. Once again the convention drew attention to the great economic inequalities in Canada and declared that political democracy would not be fully achieved until the people had a voice in administering the economic affairs of the nation, which were till then almost entirely in the hands of private interests solely concerned with profits. This profit-seeking, combined with a complete lack of economic planning and an inadequate educational system, contributed in large part to a waste of our natural resources.

I had made the fifteen-hundred-mile drive from Montreal to Winnipeg in my car with some of our other delegates. One evening, we stopped for dinner at a restaurant in Duluth, Minnesota, near the Canadian border. Hearing us speak French, a young man of about thirty came over from a nearby table to offer us a bottle of wine. Born in the United States of Quebec parents, he could not speak a word of his ancestral language. "Would you," he asked, "do my mother a great favour? She hardly ever gets a chance to speak French and if you'd phone her and tell her you're from Quebec, I'm sure she'd be very happy." I did so and I can still hear the delighted voice of the good lady, who could scarcely believe her ears. There were other incidents of a more humdrum sort. We were stopped on several occasions for speeding. Once when the police had taken us before a justice of the peace, Michel Chartrand, who had been at the wheel remarked, "Of all the hundreds of cars on the road, you would have to stop the one with a Quebec licence plate." The learned magistrate did not much appreciate this remark and fined us fifteen dollars.

On my way back from Winnipeg, I left my passengers at the railway station in North Bay and continued to Montreal alone. At a turning in a country road, I saw a police car. I followed it, increasing in speed as it did. Suddenly the policeman stopped and signalled me to do likewise. Approaching, he asked why I was driving so fast. I replied that I had believed this was quite all right since I was following him. "Lady," he said, "you have no business following the police unless they tell you to." And he too gave me a heavy fine. I thought sadly that it would have been cheaper to go to Winnipeg by train.

After our successive election defeats, the provincial council of the PSD believed it would be useful to unite under the same banner all those who wished to establish a truly democratic regime in Quebec. Maurice Duplessis was still in power but it was becoming evident that a growing number of electors had had more than enough of his totalitarianism. So the PSD organized a meeting with the aim of bringing together all those who opposed the Duplessis regime. It was to be held in the hall of the *Fédération Saint-Jean-Baptiste* on the 14th of April, 1956. As well as members of the PSD, the meeting attracted discontented liberals, trade unionists, and sympathizers, such as Pierre Trudeau, Jean Marchand, Maurice Sauvé, Pierre Dansereau, and Gérard Pelletier, and members of the *Ligue d'action socialiste*, which had been founded in 1955 by a group that wanted an organization run solely by Quebeckers. The meeting was under the joint chairmanship of Pierre Trudeau and Jacques Perreault. After considerable discussion it was decided:

1. that another meeting should be held to draw up a constitution and lay the foundations of what all had agreed to call not a political party but a movement to promote a truly democratic society that would be able to find solutions to the political, economic, and social problems of the day;

2. to establish a method of financing that would ensure the independence of action of the movement so that it could devote itself entirely to the common good;

3. to work to obtain respect for the right of all classes of society and specifically to seek the support of the workers and their participation in public affairs.

The second meeting took place on the 23rd of June and two and a half months later, on the 8th of September, 1956, the *Rassemblement provincial des citoyens* was launched. As had been understood at the spring meeting, the association was defined as a movement for education and democratic action dedicated to the protection of the fundamental rights of citizens. Branches were established in Montreal, Quebec City, Ottawa, Val d'Or, and Saint-Hyacinthe. Everyone was eligible to join, whatever his politics, if he accepted the statement of principles laid down in the constitution. Unfortunately, the organization had a relatively ephemeral existence of only three years. Even though its base was very broad, it was a heterogeneous group of people holding often divergent views. As a result, there was almost constant tension between those who gave priority to social problems and those who were primarily Quebec nationalists. Furthermore, the more doctrinaire elements opposed those who might be called pragmatists. The regulation that aimed to keep the organization apolitical, or at least not make it a party, became almost impossible to follow, for everyone had very definite political ideas, and constantly expressed them.

The *Rassemblement* had only three presidents. Pierre Dansereau, then Dean of Law at the *Université de Montréal*, René Tremblay, a professor at Laval and later a federal minister, and Pierre Elliott Trudeau. At that period, Trudeau had the reputation of being rather a dilettante and, despite his first-rate intelligence, lacking in perseverance. He was fond of launching ideas or movements only to lose interest and turn to something else. This attitude, from which he has now recovered, I trust, probably had something to do with the collapse of the *Rassemblement*. While he was president, he took a trip overseas and when he returned the *Rassemblement* no longer existed. Nevertheless, at a moment when minds were beginning to awaken in Quebec, the movement created a forum where citizens anxious for reform could meet and establish dialogue. It thus helped prepare the way for the Quiet Revolution of 1960.

Meanwhile I was carrying on the fight as leader of the PSD. In the 1957 federal election, I ran as candidate in the riding of Villeneuve, which included the town of Rouyn, a mining centre where, on one occasion, I had to take part in an all-candidate debate before an audience made up largely of miners. I admit that my being a woman and a "frightful bourgeois" as well made me feel somewhat timid. Before the meeting, I recall, I told Réal Caouette, the Créditiste candidate, that I hoped I would be heard to the end. He assured me amiably that I had nothing to fear from him since he knew I was sincere, adding with a mischievous smile that he would not be so gentle with the other two candidates, a Conservative and a Liberal. He kept his word and I have very pleasant memories of that evening. This time it was the Liberal who was elected.

The climate is harsh in the Rouyn-Noranda region, and one

can see a great many abandoned farms, for the short growing season makes them unprofitable. However, the mining industry has attracted a considerable population, come in part from the larger centres in search of a new and better life. Thus I sometimes encountered former city-dwellers of my acquaintance who expressed nostalgia for the metropolis.

There is a good deal of discussion about the reasons for the success of Social Credit in this area of northern Quebec. The people were disillusioned after all the unfulfilled promises of the traditional parties and the lack of any real improvement in their difficult lives. Réal Caouette, with his gifts as a popular speaker and the strange monetary theories of Social Credit, managed to make them believe in the promise of a better world. He became the leader of the *Ralliement des créditistes*, which, while continuing to support the economic doctrines of Social Credit, differs slightly from the Social Crediters in the rest of Canada. Another phenomenon that must be included in this context is the success in this part of the world of the *Berets blancs*. These white berets are the badge of a movement headed by Mr. Louis Even and Mrs. Gilberte Côté-Mercier that preaches a monetary theory strongly tinged with religiosity; *Vers Demain* is their official organ. Mr. Caouette, like many others, had to disassociate himself from them. The *Berets blancs* have engaged for several years in an intense propaganda campaign on radio programs and in their monthly journal. In this way they have reached a rather naive and disadvantaged segment of the population; their disciples are distinguished chiefly by their fanaticism and their intransigence.

At a meeting of the Canadian Institute of International Affairs some fifteen years ago, I made the acquaintance of a young labour leader, Jean-Robert Ouellette, the vice president of the CTCC, a man of imposing stature and serious mien who made extremely pertinent observations on several occasions. When I pointed out that it would be excellent to have a trade unionist of this calibre in our ranks, I was assured that approaching him would be a waste of time since he was a former *Créditiste* candidate. Despite this warning, I spoke to him of the interest aroused by his presence at the CIIA. He told me that he remembered the 1930s when his father, an unemployed miner, had searched desperately for work to provide adequate food for his eight children, and his mother often used to do without bread to give it to them. He himself had gone to work when he was eleven. Into this setting came the teachings of Louis Even and Gilberte Côté-Mercier. Putting his hope in their ideas as in a divine message, he worked without pay for two years selling subscriptions to *Vers Demain*. And so it was that he later became a *Créditiste* candidate. I told him about the party of which I was leader and asked him if he would read our program and tell me whether he found it interesting. I duly sent him the information and three weeks later he telephoned to say that he had not known of our party before and found it the solution to the problems that troubled him. Shortly thereafter, he joined our ranks and even became one of our candidates. He came to our national convention in Winnipeg after attending the provincial convention in Saskatchewan, the province considered the laboratory of socialism in Canada. The democratic nature of the Douglas administration and the role permitted to the party members had impressed Mr. Ouellette greatly, especially when the members challenged the ministers and did not hesitate to offer precise suggestions for improvements in the services offered by their departments. "Such a thing could never happen in Quebec," he told me, reminding me of Pierre Trudeau's remark after he had been present as an observer at a CCF convention in Toronto, "I never thought I would see such an example of democracy in action on American soil."

As I prepared for the provincial convention to be held in Shawinigan in the fall of 1957, I made up my mind to resign as leader in favour of Michel Chartrand, who was then also a member of the national council and had held a number of posts in the provincial sector. I was well aware that many people attributed our lack of electoral success to the fact that I was a woman. Others, however, were far from sharing this opinion. A great many of the members at the convention refused even to hear of my resignation, but I held to my decision. Today I have the melancholy satisfaction of feeling that they were right and that it was perhaps while I was at the head of the PSD that the party obtained most publicity and was most highly considered.

One of our guest speakers at this convention was Mr. Douglas

Fisher, the CCF candidate who had just defeated the Minister of Transport, Mr. C. D. Howe. The new member of the Commons was a good-natured giant who, until his arrival in the House, seemed not to have the faintest idea of the meaning of the "French fact" in Canada. To introduce him to this idea was one of our reasons for inviting him. Of course there was also some element of curiosity, for we wanted to have a close look at the man who had just beaten so important a minister as C. D. Howe.

I had chaired the convention in Port Arthur at which Mr. Fisher had been chosen CCF candidate and had been so impressed with him that when I returned to Ottawa to make my report to the national office, I predicted that he would be victorious in the coming struggle. Everyone had smiled incredulously, but while Mr. Howe travelled around the country and occupied himself with the affairs of his Department, Mr. Fisher spoke regularly on television and took part in a great many meetings. Also, he had the immense advantage, so much appreciated today, of being young and very close to the people. (When the results of the polling were known, I was strongly tempted whenever I chanced to meet members of the national office to remind them of my prediction.)

In the next federal election, held on the 31st of March, 1958, the CCF suffered serious reverses. On this occasion I ran once more in Jacques-Cartier-Lasalle, where my Conservative opponent was John Pratt, the mayor of Dorval. During an inter-party debate, he was kind enough to say that if he had not been running against me, he would have voted for me. I must say that whenever I did run for election, my opponents were always most courteous. However, I lost once again and Mr. John Pratt went to sit in Ottawa with more than two hundred other Conservatives. My party won only eight seats, the lowest figure since 1940.

After this Conservative sweep, it became very clear that the participation of labour in Canadian political life must cease to be merely a matter of abstract discussion. Canada needed a party with a labour base that would be strong enough to become one of the two principal parliamentary groups. As a result, at the annual meeting of the Canadian Labour Congress in April 1958, one of the matters under discussion was whether the congress should finally take a position with a view to entering politics. There appeared to be two choices: either provide massive support for the CCF or form a new party. As Stanley Knowles wrote in *The New Party*:

> The Convention passed its now historic resolution, which was welcomed by the CCF at the National Convention later that same year, calling for a fundamental political realignment through the creation of a broadly based political movement embracing the CCF, the labour movement, farm organizations, professional people, and other liberally minded persons interested in basic social reform and reconstruction through our parliamentary system of government Thus the idea of the New Party became a fact in Canadian politics.[4]

The same resolution was submitted to a CCF convention held in Regina in July, 1958. It gave rise to a good deal of discussion, and I remember the particularly impressive statement of a speaker who recalled the services rendered to Canada by the trade union movement for over a century and the devotion of the CCF to the welfare of the Canadian people for more than twenty-five years. His speech concluded: "No power on earth can stop us, for our movements are united and other movements will surely join with us to work tirelessly for the common good, the dignity of man, and world peace." I chaired the meeting at which the resolution, put to the vote in the two languages, was unanimously adopted. With this mandate, the national committee settled down to work. It was decided that a convention should be held in Ottawa, the capital of Canada, from the 31st of July to the 4th of August, 1961. In this way, the New Democratic Party was founded. It was, in effect, a modernized CCF. For three days, hundreds of delegates assembled in the Coliseum drew up a program that would meet the needs of the future. It was established at the outset that even though the CCF had never formed a government, it had made its presence deeply felt and had inspired a great many social measures that Canadians enjoyed. It was now a question of attacking new problems such as housing, medicare, and economic planning to ensure that the immense natural resources of the country would be put to the best possible use. During this initial convention, there were some rather violent discussions about the status of Quebec. The Quebec delegation was sharply divided, for on the labour side there were echoes of the Champigny convention and signs of the separatist tendencies that still create so many difficulties among our people. These delegates objected to the use of the word "federal" in the phrasing of various resolutions and wanted the convention to recognize the right of every province to self-determination. As Donald MacDonald, newly elected leader of Ontario remarked, "Despite the adjective federal, the party is national in scope and we will work to make it so."

There were also a series of discussions about the choice of a name for this new political movement. I was one of those who opposed "the New Party," since I believed that this name would lose its whole point with time and that it gave no indication of the principles uniting us. I should have preferred "Social Democratic Party," which truly reflected our ideology, but it was argued that the existence of a Democratic party in the United States might lead to confusion. Eventually the name New Democratic Party was chosen by the majority of votes and passed into history.

The convention concluded with the election of a leader and a national council. Mr. Tommy Douglas, the former premier of Saskatchewan, became the first national leader of the NDP. The outgoing CCF leader, M. J. Coldwell, retired but remained the respected counsellor, loved by all. I was elected to the national council and had the satisfaction of seeing created the new position of French-speaking co-chairman of the council. The members from the various provinces then proceeded to form their own branches of the NDP. This took place much later in Quebec for, despite the efforts of some of us, dissensions among the Quebec candidates continued very strong.

During the provincial elections of 1960, I felt that we should once again field a great many candidates. Our leader, Michel Chartrand, did not share my opinion but tried instead to join forces with the Liberals to defeat the *Union nationale*. He had little success and once again our few candidates bit the dust. The new Liberal leader, Mr. Jean Lesage and his so-called *équipe du tonnerre* came to power and so began what was known as the Quiet Revolution. One of the team was René Lévesque, who was already known as a CBC reporter; his program, *Point de mire* had attracted thousands of viewers in the province. He had also played a leading role in the CBC strike a few years before. A sincere and dynamic man, he inspired confidence in his public and had the common touch. It is undeniable that he contributed largely to the Liberal victory. Mr. Lesage had a more polished style and his speeches were more substantial, but he was more distant. I once heard a worker say of him that he was a fine man and a good speaker but so "high hat" that you couldn't even approach him.

Once the Liberals were in power, René Lévesque was named Minister of Natural Resources. In less than two years he managed to persuade his colleagues to nationalize the provincial hydro system, a measure that the *Action libérale* and the CCF had urged for many years. Public ownership of electric power, which had already existed in Ontario for forty years, was a very important step for Quebec. Here, as so many times before, our province lagged terribly far behind and we were again paying dearly for the ultra-conservatism of the past. It is known, for instance, that Taschereau resisted the granting of old age pensions for a decade on the excuse that our people had enough heart to look after their own old parents. The results were often pathetic; old people who had given all they had to their children were harshly treated in return and were in some cases even left destitute. In another sector, there was still no wage parity and our teachers were very poorly paid.

This accumulation of measures taken too late or not at all goes a long way to explain the success of such men as René Lévesque. He sometimes has excellent ideas but to obtain his objectives he exploits the frustrations arising from the errors of the past, often offering dubious solutions. For him economic considerations, however essential, seem to be of secondary importance. One day, I asked him, "What are you doing from the economic point of view?" He answered, "We'll speak of that afterwards," probably meaning after Quebec becomes independent. I replied that it would be much better to speak of it before.

I do not agree with those members of the *Parti québécois* who advocate unilingualism. Indeed, is it not incredible to imagine, in a world that is being drawn ever more closely together by communications, that Quebec, with its five million or so French-speaking inhabitants, could exert any influence whatever in a continent of two hundred and fifty million English-speaking people if these five million spoke only French? If Quebec wishes to flourish, it can do so only by encouraging its people to acquire a competence and dynamism that will impress outsiders. Nor should it be forgotten that immigrants who have come to Quebec in search of a better life may not choose to remain in that province forever.

XIII

Around the World in Eighty Days

As a very little girl I had read Jules Verne's *Le Tour du monde en quatre-vingts jours*, never dreaming then that fifty years later I myself would embark on a similar journey.

In 1956 I left Montreal for Bombay, India, to represent the CCF at a congress of the Socialist Nations of Asia for Mr. M. J. Coldwell, the leader of our party, who had been obliged to go to Sweden. Before my departure, Pierre Elliott Trudeau had asked whether I would consent to have his mother accompany me since he did not want her to travel alone, especially in Asia. I accepted with pleasure. My own children had had similar fears for me and my friend, Miss Madeleine Tourville, had agreed to go along. After a brief stay in Paris, the three of us proceeded to Rome where we were to catch a flight to India. Our ambassador to Italy, Mr. Pierre Dupuy, was kind enough to drive us in person to the airport.

Towards eight o'clock in the evening, we set out for Cairo aboard a TCA plane. All was going smoothly when suddenly, at about ten o'clock, there was a very violent and frightening thunderstorm. A few minutes later the pilot announced that we would have to land in Athens. We believed that this was the result of the storm, for the airport was in total darkness. We were requested, by candlelight, to surrender our passports and our money–which were returned to us on departure–and taken by bus to a hotel. Not till the next morning, when we noticed the beautifully embroidered sheets on our beds, did we realize that we were at the luxurious Astir Hotel, the most modern in Athens. After breakfasting on the terrace, which gave us a view of the sea, I telephoned our embassy to find out how we could continue our journey. Since the ambassador was on vacation, there was only a chargé d'affaires to look after us. To our amazement we learned later that morning that Israel had marched on Egypt the evening before and the two countries were now at war. This was the real reason for our stop at Athens. The delay was serious for me since the congress I was to attend in India was already in session. However, my disappointment was alleviated in part by this opportunity to see the city and its surroundings. The weather was splendid and I shall never forget the wonderful view from the Acropolis, so white against the luminous blue sky, with Athens and the Gulf of Aegina spread out at our feet.

After three days of exploring this enchanting city, we were able to return to Rome to continue to India by another route. When we made a short stop at Teheran, rain was falling in great torrents and the suspicious Persians eyed us more or less kindly, not knowing on which side of the present conflict our sympathies lay. Dawn found us in Karachi in Pakistan, where we had to change planes. The heat was dry and scorching and everything seemed desolate and sad. To cheer us up, a priest who had shared our journey said, "Courage, ladies! The first time I was here, it nearly killed me, but you eventually get used to it!" After all these adventures we finally reached Bombay, where the congress had been underway for six days.

I was installed in a beautiful suite in the Taj Mahal Hotel and everyone, delegates and hotel-employees alike, did their utmost to make the representative of Canada forget the problems she had encountered en route. Striking contrasts constantly drew our attention and aroused our pity. For instance, at our hotel, which was built all of white marble, the ground floor window sills served at night as beds for poor wretches who had nowhere else to sleep, and in the evening the neighbouring streets were completely covered with homeless people stretched out one beside the other, making it impossible to drive. Whenever we went out, beggars ran toward us, crying, "Baksheesh! Baksheesh!" The deep blue of the ocean, the lush vegetation, and the whiteness of the buildings sparkling in the dazzling sun could not make us forget such poverty, whose horrors we could never have imagined.

The congress, under the chairmanship of U Nu, Prime Minister of Burma, had brought together a great many delegates and observers from all parts of Asia and Africa. Among the most distinguished were Mr. Asotha Metha, the President of the Social Democratic party of India, and Mr. Bandaranaike, the Prime Minister of Ceylon. The delegate of Kenya, Mr. Murumbi, particularly caught my attention by his advanced ideas and brilliant way of expressing his point of view. A man of imposing stature, he wore a little gold cross at his neck, proudly indicating his adherence to the Catholic Church. He had first gone to a school run by nuns, who were so struck by his talents that they sent him to continue his education in London. The English were so afraid of his possible influence on his people that they would not permit him to return to Kenya; the Americans refused him entry into the United States. Even so, he was representing his country at the congress and, after it achieved independence, he became Minister of Foreign Affairs and ambassador to the United Nations in New York.

All the delegates were intensely nationalistic and the discussions dealt chiefly with problems of education and economics. On the last evening, there was an extraordinary assembly of some fifty thousand people in one of the large parks of Bombay. The audience sat on the ground, Indian-fashion, listening with deep attention. Murumbi mounted the rostrum and explained that his country had no money to offer but would supply books, pens, and paper. "Education," he said, "is absolutely necessary for a people that wants to obtain its freedom." In the name of the CCF I, in my turn, offered my best wishes for success to all the delegates and expressed the admiration of Canada for these peoples who wished to educate themselves and to throw off the yoke that weighed them down.

Before leaving Bombay, I dined one evening at the home of Mr. Nehru's youngest sister, the wife of a very wealthy man who represented Lever Brothers in India. Pretty, charming, and intelligent, she had the outspokenness of Nehru and his daughter, Indira Gandhi, and was considered the *enfant terrible* of the family. Although not as famous as her sister, Mme. Pandit, she was known in her own right for the articles that she had written for various English and American publications.

After the congress, I was invited to spend a few days in New Delhi with our High Commissioner, Mr. Escott Reid, and his wife, who received me warmly and showed me the city and its surroundings. I had the privilege to visit and admire, under a bright sun as well as by moonlight, the glittering Taj Mahal in the magnificent setting of its flower-filled gardens to which respectful pilgrims, both rich and poor, flock in their hundreds. At a sitting of Lok Sabba, the Indian Parliament, I heard Nehru speak several times in English during a debate and later, at an official celebration, I was introduced to him and his daughter, Indira Gandhi. During my stay, my hosts also gave a dinner party for me inviting several prominent people, including the Minister of Health, who was a woman.

My next stop was Ceylon where I renewed acquaintance with Mr. Bandaranaike whose sense of humour had so entertained us at the Bombay congress. One day, he stood up in his severe national costume, similar to that of our secular clergy, and announced solemnly in an English accent straight from Oxford, "I am going to make a speech that is like a woman's dress, long enough to cover the subject and short enough to make it interesting." Coming from an Asian, this somewhat stale joke was quite surprising. His wife, then president of the International Women's Institute, received us graciously, delighted to acquaint westerners with the charm of eastern hospitality. Barely a year later, her husband was assassinated almost on the doorstep of their house and Mrs. Bandaranaike succeeded him as prime minister.

The next day we left Colombo for Kandy, where we visited the university. As we crossed the campus we were able to admire the numerous Sinhalese beauties in their multicoloured saris, all with no other thought, it seemed, but succeeding in their courses. Canada had given Ceylon a considerable sum of money to build a hydro-electric dam; this surely helped warm the people of the country toward us and we were sad to have to take our leave. In response to an invitation from Prime Minister U Nu during the congress, I flew next to Rangoon in Burma. As I passed through immigration at five in the morning, I was behind two important looking gentlemen, a well-dressed American carrying a very large briefcase and a moustached Englishman bundled into a checked overcoat. Suddenly the official beckoned me forward. "You're a Canadian, Madame? Pass right through please." And turning to the others, he added in a peremptory tone, "Just wait where you are." The two gentlemen were obviously both surprised and shocked.

I had just checked in at my hotel and was looking forward to a well-earned rest when the telephone rang; the Prime Minister's secretary wished to know if I would like to attend a sitting of the Assembly which was just about to begin. When I expressed my willingness, he replied "Good, I'll be right over," and then explained that the intense noonday heat forced parliament to sit very early in the morning. As I entered the hall, I saw the Prime Minister on the dais, surrounded by his cabinet. "You're late," he said, and I replied that this was the fault of the plane and not mine. I took a seat among an audience of fifteen hundred Burmese dressed in long white tunics with red sashes; never was I so conscious of my white skin and blue eyes. After the sitting, at about ten o'clock, U Nu very graciously arranged for me to tour the parliament building.

Rangoon is a most attractive city with a great many shining gold minarets and colourful flower-markets. At the state radio building, I met a technician who told me he had studied in Ottawa and seemed delighted to meet a Canadian. After a visit to the very modern university, I had dinner with two charming professors, husband and wife, the former a member of the Burmese delegation to the Bombay congress. During the meal I noticed some small lizards walking gaily about on the ceiling and, despite myself, kept raising my eyes, fearful of seeing one of them fall onto my plate. My hosts put my mind at rest when they then explained that these reptiles were very useful since they fed on mosquitoes, whose bites are very painful. Shortly afterwards I was offered the chance to visit Mandalay, some two hundred and fifty miles from Rangoon, provided I informed the authorities, who would furnish a military escort to protect me from possible attacks by rebels along the way. This prospect left me cold and I declined.

Before my departure, the Minister of Foreign Affairs called me to his office and asked me to take an important and confidential message to the Prime Minister of Canada. He explained that the

USSR had a diplomatic representative in Burma who was actively engaged in propaganda. At that time, neither Britain nor France was very popular with the Burmese who, as a result, would have liked to see a Canadian ambassador come and play a major role in their country. I passed this suggestion along to Mr. St. Laurent as soon as I returned to Canada, and he seemed very sympathetic to the idea. However, his government was defeated shortly afterwards and our country still has no ambassador in Rangoon.

My next visit, to Thailand, had nothing official about it. Bangkok, the capital, with its many dazzling minarets, has a wonderful pagoda of multicoloured porcelain that houses an emerald Buddha. In the streets, a great many Buddhist monks with shaved heads and saffron robes wander along seeking alms. In order to appreciate fully the spectacle of the floating markets, we took a little boat through the various small canals where vegetables, fruit, and flowers are displayed on barges, while a motley crowd haggles over them with great excitement. Sometimes in the enthusiasm of a transaction a customer tumbles into the water and everyone rushes to fish him out.

From Bangkok we went to Hong Kong, where we stayed for about ten days. This port, which is wide open to the West, is only a few miles from Red China. The English exercise benevolent control over it, which suits the Peking government perfectly; if it did not, they could easily put an end to this. The stores are bursting with beautiful merchandise at very tempting prices. Labour is very poorly paid; otherwise, how could things be sold so cheaply, even in the absence of excise taxes? In this over-populated city, especially in the poorer neighbourhoods, live thousands of refugees from Red China, and it is difficult to know the political allegiance of each one of them. On a white marble building on Commercial Street, I was astonished to read these words, *Communist Bank of China*, and thought that perhaps all our different political ideologies are to some extent simply a matter of semantics.

The beauty of the Eurasian women is remarkable. With an Indian guide, I visited Repulse Bay, where the American film based on Han Suyin's *A Many Splendoured Thing* was made. Hong Kong offers an extraordinary spectacle with its innumerable junks, each the home for an entire family. Drinking water is scarce and is cut off completely for certain hours of the day. The traveller is struck by the unbelievable number of cockroaches; we even found them in the chest of drawers. I could never bring myself to use one of the rickshaws that wretched coolies drag up the steep hills of the city for a few cents a trip. And yet, dominated by a mountain covered with expensive white houses, Hong Kong is surely one of the most beautiful and interesting cities one could ever hope to see. The natural setting and the climate are magnificent.

Our departure from Hong Kong gave us one or two anxious moments; the aircraft paused like a gigantic bird at the very edge of the bay, its motor throbbing as we waited for a suitable wind for takeoff. To an American passenger who became irritated because we weren't moving, one of the officers replied, "Sir, don't you think it's better to take our time than take a nose-dive into the ocean?"

A few hours later we were in Tokyo where we were met by a delegation of Japanese socialist members of the Diet and by Mr. Gilles Lalande, the first secretary, representing our ambassador, and today a professor at the *Université de Montréal*. We were driven to the celebrated Imperial Hotel, the only building left standing after the earthquake of 1923, where our rooms, which were in the older part of the hotel, were most luxurious. However, as westerners used to certain modern conveniences and services, we found other things quite strange. Tokyo has a population of about ten million, but the names of streets are not marked and it is a real headache to find your way about. Taxis travel at insane speeds and are nicknamed *Kamikaze*, after those pilots of the last war who used to commit suicide by diving into enemy ships. Though I am not fearful by nature, I never went into the streets without feeling some apprehension.

I was invited to a meeting of the socialist parliamentary committee, where international problems were under discussion. Rightly or wrongly, I had a vague impression that there is very little love among the Japanese for the white race. Their attitude toward Americans, though perfectly correct, remains impenetrable. Knowing that I had been a member of the Japanese-Canadian committee during the last war, my hosts did everything they could to make my stay pleasant and I was asked to thank one of our members of parliament, Angus MacInnis of Vancouver, who had founded the association. His widow, Grace MacInnis, is the only woman member of the House of Commons at the present time. From her father, J. S. Woodsworth, she inherited great intelligence, sound judgment, and a deep love for her fellow man. In Japan, I could not help but be struck by the number of women members in the Senate and Diet.

I telephoned an old friend from my convent days, the Mother Superior of the Convent of the Sacred Heart in Tokyo, Mother Valérie Metayer. The school has more than six hundred pupils, and among its most illustrious graduates are the Japanese crown princess and Mrs. Kato, the wife of a Japanese ambassador to Ottawa. My friend, who had lived in the country for twenty-five years, told me that she had spent the duration of the war in a concentration camp and that one of the most distressing features of the prisoners' lives was the complete absence of news.

One evening, a woman member of the Diet invited me to one of the most elegant clubs in Tokyo for an authentic Japanese meal. I perhaps did not appreciate some of the more exotic dishes as much as she did, the raw fish, for instance. In Kyoto, we toured the famous palace of the emperors and the gardens, most of whose trees were wrapped in a sort of cotton batting to protect them from the November frost. The huge rooms of the palace, which were hung with beautiful paintings but without furniture or carpets, gave us an impression of coldness and walking through them without shoes did little to warm our enthusiasm.

To see heavy industry we had to go to Osaka, the future site of Expo 70. While we listened to the piped-in music, our train travelled at a dizzying speed. The cars were exceedingly clean; every quarter of an hour stewardesses came along and dusted the windows. When I asked, "What's there to see in Osaka?", the young socialist party secretary who was acting as my guide replied, "Well, if you have to choose, I'd advise you to go and see the factories. The temples are beautiful but when you've seen one you've seen them all." My interest in social questions made me inclined to follow his advice and we visited National Electric, which manufactures everything from pocket flashlights to transformers.

The directors of the company welcomed us with many bows and took us to the boardroom where we were offered hot tea and steaming towels to wash our hands. After telling us how financially successful the company was, one of the directors took us through the plant, where five thousand unionized employees were working with quite remarkable speed and skill, not even raising their eyes as we passed. They worked an eight-hour day, but I still do not know their hourly wage, for each time I raised the question my attention was drawn to one or another of the products being made. As we were leaving, we were presented with small portable radios much better made than many others I have seen.

The president of the Osaka socialist committee, a quite tall man and the very image of a western businessman, wished to entertain us. When he asked what we would like to see that evening, I expressed the desire to visit a geisha house. He agreed to my suggestion and called for us that evening, clad now in the traditional kimona, and took us to a house where the hostess received us very courteously. Middle-aged, she spoke English fluently and was able to converse with us on all the questions of the day. Seated on cushions on the floor with a brazier at our feet, we were served boiling saké in minuscule cups and then two little geishas were brought in. They were about fifteen years old, with truly doll-like expressionless faces whitened with powder, clad in elegant white kimonas embroidered in bright colors with contrasting obis, and with flowers tucked just so in their dark coiffures. They sang and talked for a moment in hesitant English. Then our hostess begged us to excuse them since in view of their youth and the lateness of the hour they must be taken home. For us this unusual evening was fascinating.

Next day in Tokyo our Canadian ambassador, Mr. T. C. Davis, who had been a member of parliament at the same time as my husband, entertained us very graciously in his residence, one of the most beautiful in the city. Now on our journey homeward, we had to make a refuelling stop at Wake, a tiny island lost in the Pacific Ocean. Though it was night, it was too hot even to think of stirring. A feeling of distress gripped me when I saw the board listing the distances between Wake and the rest of the universe. What a relief it was to arrive in Honolulu and to feel that I was back once more in a world that was familiar. It was December but so mild that we were able to eat dinner on the terrace in light dresses, watching visitors from the four corners of the globe dancing in magnificent moonlight. I thought of my own country, where I would soon be again, so icy cold and snow-covered at this season. At Pearl Harbor we could see the tops of the American ships that had been sunk in the first enemy raid during the war. There was a Japanese in our group of tourists and I can still remember his expression when he heard the guide say that the Nippons had paid dearly for their attack of that day.

Vancouver was the last stop on our homeward journey. On arrival we were told that a tragic accident two evenings before had taken the lives of about fifty passengers en route to eastern Canada. And we had the same flight number! Then came the announcement that engine trouble would delay our takeoff for several hours. Despite all these hitches, we arrived next day safe and sound, in time to celebrate Christmas with our families.

XIV

No More War

I had long been persuaded that women could contribute a particular sort of energy to the establishment of peace, and in February, 1961, I resolved to found a Quebec branch of the Voice of Women. The previous year, as a result of the U-2 incident, the Paris summit conference had broken down, and relations between the United States and Russia reached a low ebb.[1] Some Ontario women then appealed to all the women of Canada to speak out against the tensions of the cold war and the imminent threat of nuclear conflict. Their objective was to ensure peace through negotiation and the application of their motto: "Construction, not destruction." When I learned of the meeting at Maple Leaf Gardens in Toronto at which the winner of the Nobel prize for peace, Noel Baker, spoke very eloquently, I immediately got in touch with Mrs. Helen Tucker, the president of the new movement, and told her of my intention to organize a branch in Quebec. Several women met at my home, among others Senator Marianna Jodoin, who had worked with me in the old days in the struggle to obtain the provincial vote. I was elected president of our branch and Senator Jodoin honorary president.

French-Canadian women shared with their English-speaking fellow-countrywomen a love for children and family life, the very basis of society. Knowing that the men could not accomplish enough on their own, we decided to join with them to combat the threat of nuclear and biological warfare, and to arouse feelings of sympathy and understanding among the general public. Mrs. Lester Pearson gave the movement her support from its inception[2] and in the first issue of our bulletin she wrote: " . . . If we, the women of the West, could succeed in reaching women of the other side of the curtain with no political overtones, but only as the mothers

of young children whose lives are at stake under this threat. . .
I think we could start a chain reaction toward peace instead of
war."

At the end of our first month's work, our Quebec branch had
recruited more than a hundred members. Despite their varying
political opinions, all were united in the common cause of peace.
We studied the effects of radiation, international affairs, ways to
relieve world tension, disarmament, and peace. In March, 1961,
a Montreal delegation went by special train to Ottawa to present
a brief to the Prime Minister, the Honourable John Diefenbaker.
This document contained nothing new on the subject of peace,
but the Voice of Women wanted to let the government know that
at least one segment of the public was well informed. Mr. Diefenbaker and five other ministers received us in the railway committee
room in Parliament; the Honourable Léon Balcer, Minister of
Transport, replied to the questions of those who spoke French.
The delegates then went to see their respective members of parliament before returning home. The press, radio, and television gave
a great deal of coverage to our action, and our membership, both
male and female, increased considerably throughout the country.
Many men had encouraged their wives to go to Ottawa with us,
even offering to look after the children themselves during their
absence. It was during this trip that Solange Chaput-Rolland and
Gwendolyn Graham met and decided to collaborate on their book,
Chers ennemis (Dear Enemies), which was such a success in 1963.

In March, 1962, the Voice of Women sent Mrs. Ghislaine Laurendeau, Mrs. Raymonde Roy, and myself to Geneva to join with
a delegation from Women's Strike for Peace of the United States
to present our demands to the international committee on disarmament then in session. Most of the delegates received us warmly;
those of the USSR and the United States were more reserved.
Perhaps the fact that they possessed nuclear weapons made them
harder to convince of the merits of our demands. Mr. Green,
the Canadian Minister for External Affairs, had very kindly given
us the assistance of his staff to prepare the documents we wished
to present. On one occasion, we had lunch with Mrs. Alva Myrdal,
the Swedish ambassador, who was her country's delegate. She was
a most intelligent and friendly as well as a very pretty woman.

Mr. Green told me that she had often succeeded in creating a better atmosphere between the Soviet and American delegates. We also had the privilege of a short interview with U Thant, the Secretary General of the United Nations, who urged us to continue our work. At about eleven o'clock that evening his chauffeur brought hot coffee to the women of the delegation who were maintaining a vigil before the *Palais des Nations*.

We then went on to Vienna to be present as observers at a congress of the Federation of Democratic Women, a somewhat left-wing organization whose members, however, were generally willing to listen to different points of view during the discussions. Some fifty countries had sent delegates to the congress, which was under the chairmanship of Mrs. Eugénie Coton, a former member of the French National Assembly, to which she had been elected in 1944, immediately after the liberation. Though now quite elderly, she exercised great authority but always in a democratic way. The Russian delegation was headed by a member of the editorial board of *Pravda*, who as a journalist had often lived abroad, notably in Paris and Saigon. At that time, relations between the People's Republic of China and the USSR seemed excellent. One day I noticed that my neighbour at table, the Chinese delegate who was also a minister in the Peking government, was looking at me with marked coldness; she doubtless considered me the prime product of capitalism, the bourgeoisie, and the Catholic Church. As we couldn't converse in our respective languages, I tried to lessen our apparent lack of mutual understanding by showing her my grandmother bracelet engraved with the names of my numerous grandchildren and then taking their pictures out of my purse. Her face lit up with a beautiful smile as she showed me in turn a photo of two Chinese youngsters. From that moment, we were the best of friends, offering one another smiles and greetings on every occasion. Such contacts always reminded me that human beings, on the whole, are the same all over the world.

The evening before we left, we had dinner with the ambassador of the USSR. We were seated at a lavishly appointed table and our meal, which had nothing Russian about it but a delicious borsch, was served by charming young girls in minuscule aprons. Our host told amusing stories that illustrated the keen sense of humour of his people. At the end of the evening, he sent us back in his car and I shall never forget the shocked look on the door-man's face when he saw the chauffeur shake our hands effusively before driving away.

On our return to Canada, we settled down to work again, busying ourselves with speeches, meetings, fund-raising, and the prepara-tion of briefs, reports, and press releases. Once again I was in the thick of the fray and the target for attacks from the reactionaries of our province, especially the *Action catholique*, which in their paper on the 5th of April, 1962, described Voice of Women as "falsely humanitarian and misguided in their political aims."

In the federal election that June, I ran in Outremont-Saint-Jean as a peace candidate under the auspices of the New Democratic Party. Unlike the two old parties, though they also opposed nuclear arms for Canada, the NDP had a clear, precise program which I offered to the electors, telling them to think of their children and have the courage to oppose the militarism that was sweeping the world. I also advocated Canadian recognition of the People's Republic of China, which did not mean accepting its philosophy any more than we had accepted that of the USSR. In a comment on the election, André Laurendeau wrote in *Le Devoir* that of the four candidates in Outremont "the best man—is a woman."[3] As I had no election funds, my campaign was somewhat innovative, for we had to use imagination to attract the voters' attention. It was June and we drove through the streets of Outremont with a loudspeaker. A doctor of the riding had put his car at my disposal, and seated on the hood with a string of honking cars behind, I travelled through the streets waving and smiling at everyone we passed. We had no trouble with the police but we had an impres-sion that this sort of propaganda didn't please them very much. A great many immigrants live in Outremont and I remember the pleasure of the Italian voters—who then proceeded to vote against me—when I spoke to them in their own language. Throughout the campaign, members of the VOW went from door to door, prog-ram in hand, explaining the position of the various parties on nuclear weapons. The fact that I ran as a peace candidate opposed to nuclear arms for Canada won me a great deal of sympathy, but not enough to carry the day. There were more than three hundred polling stations in the riding. The old parties paid their scrutineers fifteen or twenty dollars each and brought them hot lunches. Ours didn't receive a cent and felt that they were merely serving their country. I noticed that when the women saw me enter a poll and remembered my fight to obtain the female vote, they seemed ashamed of being against me. Since I had already known defeat, I was in a familiar situation. I received 4,308 votes, which was more than ever before, except in my 1942 campaign.

In September, about fifty women from seventeen countries came to Canada to attend a peace conference organized by Voice of Women. The aims of the conference were twofold – to gain worldwide support for the idea that the United Nations dedicate a year to international cooperation and to obtain a nuclear test-ban. Women had long observed the failure of negotiations and thought that a *rapprochement* between the nations of the world was now possible which would allow them to work together in an atmosphere of mutual trust to halt the spreading of arms. Women were ready to take certain risks to ensure peace rather than cling to the outworn concept of national security. After several days of private meetings, a public session was held at the *Université de Montréal* at which Margaret Mead, the well-known anthropologist, expressed the belief that women, who are used to tasks requiring perseverance, are particularly fitted to work for peace. The resolutions of the annual meeting of Voice of Women, which followed the conference, dealt with the various matters under study, especially our work for peace and rejection of nuclear arms for Canada. I was elected national president, a position I held only until the next federal election – that is, for less than a year – but I had a great deal of work to accomplish during that brief period.

Shortly thereafter, in October, Russian ships, presumed to be loaded with nuclear missiles, headed for Cuba to establish military bases there. President Kennedy announced that Cuba would be blockaded and the Russian frigates halted on the high seas, and the NORAD powers were put on a state of alert. At this point, I received a phone call from Mrs. Cyrus Eaton of the American Women Strike for Peace, who told me that her organization had leased an aircraft. A delegation of members from her organization was to fly to Cuba and ask Castro not to permit the installation of nuclear bases for possible attack against the United States. She wished to know whether I would be willing, as president of the

Voice of Women, to join them on this humanitarian mission. Not only did I consent, but I also asked that another Canadian woman should go with me. She agreed and I invited Mrs. André Laurendeau, the national vice president. Understanding the need for swift action, her husband undertook to look after their six children himself. The trip was called off a few hours later, however, when we learned that Castro had agreed not to accept the weapons Khrushchev was sending and the Russian fleet was returning to its home port.

On the 25th of October, in the name of the Voice of Women, I sent the following telegram to Prime Minister Diefenbaker:

> VOW of Canada in the face of the present crisis, urges you, Mr. P.M. to (A) use all of Canada's prestige and resources to support the efforts of the acting secretary, U Thant, to mediate the current dispute, upholding the right and the authority of the United Nations as the highest arbitrator of all international disputes in the world today, and (B) to urge the president of the United States of America and chairman Khrushchev to negotiate through the United Nations since all underprivileged nations will suffer the consequences of steps taken by individual states.

On the 1st of November, a delegation from Voice of Women submitted a petition for disarmament to Mr. Zatin, the Soviet Minister of Foreign Affairs at the United Nations in New York, and in Ottawa another delegation presented a brief to the Prime Minister requesting the rejection of nuclear weapons for Canada, the immediate signing of a nuclear test-ban treaty, and the renegotiation of all treaties that implicitly drew our country into armed conflict between the nuclear powers. We had made ourselves the spokesmen for all women, all mothers and wives, who desired peace in the world for their children–peace through disarmament, negotiation, and a world law promulgated by the United Nations.

All these months, we had also kept a vigilant eye upon the defence policy of Canada. On the 30th of April, 1962, the Liberal party had stated in its political platform for the 18th of June election:

> The acquisition of nuclear weapons by additional nations can only further endanger the peace of the world .... In the light of present facts, the defence policy of a new Liberal government *will not oblige Canada to become a nuclear power by the manufacture, acquisition, or use of nuclear arms, whether under Canadian or American control.*[4]

And on the 14th of November, Mr. Pearson wrote:

> I have always maintained that nuclear powers should not be expanded and that Canadians should not accept nuclear weapons under either national control or jointly with the United States.[5]

How misleading these statements were to prove a few months later. On the 12th of January, 1963, Pearson declared suavely in a speech to the York-Scarborough Liberal Association that the Canadian government:

> ... should stop avoiding its responsibilities and immediately carry out the commitments it had made on Canada's behalf. . . . The only way to do this is to agree to accept nuclear warheads for the defensive strategic weapons that cannot be used effectively without them . . . .
> The CF-104s cannot do their full job without nuclear warheads. Neither can the Bomarc and Honest John missiles.
> As a Canadian I am ashamed when commitments are made in my name and not carried out.[6]

Such an about-face astonished the whole nation.

The resignation of the Minister of Defence, Mr. Douglas Harkness, the lack of confidence in the Diefenbaker government that followed the Cuban missile crisis and its failure to win the support of the parliamentary minorities led to its defeat in February 1963. As I had very definite ideas about peace, I decided to run again as a peace candidate in Outremont-Saint-Jean in the April election. Not wishing to embarrass the Voice of Women, which had not yet taken a position in politics, I resigned as president. The chief issue of the campaign was whether or not Canada should accept nuclear weapons. Pierre Elliott Trudeau gave a speech on my behalf, and also on behalf of Charles Taylor, in which he strongly opposed the acceptance of such weapons by our country. The Liberals emerged victorious, but only obtained a minority of seats. I was not elected but I received 4,227 votes. Pierre Trudeau published an article in *Cité Libre* entitled "Pearson, or the Abdication of the Spirit," which concluded as follows:

> I well remember the federal Liberals of 1957. They were cynics who believed that power was theirs by right and they came very close to putting Parliament under trusteeship. Six years in opposition might have had a purging effect upon them; alas, the events of the last two months have proved otherwise. I find the same brutish

cynicism among the old guard, the same self-serving docility in the youth groups; and between them are the men of my generation, quivering with anticipation because they have glimpsed the painted face of power. In the name of realism and efficiency, I have been forced at times, may God forgive me, to betray some of the rebellions of my youth. But I have not yet consented to trample on democracy. That is why I intend to vote for the New Democratic Party in the election on the 8th of April.

I think that this is the duty of everyone who considers it urgent to check the rush of Canadian political thought towards utter degradation. Government instability, the fragmentation of the opposition, the risk of "losing one's vote"–these are minor dangers compared to the abdication of the spirit to which Pearson is inviting us.[7]

I continued the fight for peace. At the end of April I went to Rome as the only Canadian representative in a world-wide pilgrimage of women's peace organizations that wished to thank Pope John XXIII for his encyclical, *Pacem in Terris*. In our delegation was a young Japanese girl who had been severely burned at Hiroshima, where her entire family had perished. To make the full horrors of war better known, some American pacifists had sent her at their expense to join her voice with ours. Through the offices of Mgr. Carew, the Canadian secretary to the Secretary of State for the Vatican, I had the privilege of visiting the Holy Father's private apartments with the Japanese girl and Mrs. Virginia Nave of American Women Strike for Peace.

All that year, the Quebec Voice of Women continued to urge Pearson not to accept nuclear weapons for Canada and to revise his defence policy, since we believed that such actions by someone who had won a Nobel prize for peace, would have great value as an example that other nations might follow. We also submitted a brief to the Commons defence committee, reiterating our positions–the rejection of nuclear arms for Canada, the renunciation of biological and chemical weapons and all other means of mass destruction, a halt to the export of all materials destined for the manufacture or maintenance of such weapons, and the immediate establishment of a program to convert a wartime economy into an economy based on peace. Demonstrating was one of our methods long before such actions became popular. We believed that collective action was a very powerful means of applying pressure, and, in fact, the only way for the masses to get themselves heard and heeded.

In May, there was a meeting of NATO in The Hague. While it was taking place some members of VOW and WISP[8] went to the Netherlands to recommend a new strategy for the establishment of peace–complete withdrawal of NATO from Central Europe and an immediate halt to the proliferation of nuclear weapons, more specifically those intended for submarines. Other women joined the delegates from North America, and about fifteen hundred of them filed silently around the building where the meeting was being held, each carrying daffodils and a placard bearing the word PEACE and a picture of her children. This demonstration received publicity all around the world.

At the invitation of Prime Minister Ben Gurion of Israel, the International Socialist Council met that November for the first time outside Europe–in the city of Haifa. I attended as the representative of the New Democratic Party. There were some very interesting people among the delegates, such as Giuseppe Saragat of Italy, Paul-Henri Spaak of Belgium, Hugh Gaitskill of England, and Guy Mollet of France. The usual questions of housing, wages, and popular education were discussed. Since the council had no power to make fundamental decisions, the delegates gave an account of what was being accomplished in various fields in their countries. Mrs. Golda Meir, then Israel's Minister of Foreign Affairs, gave an eloquent address which was received with great enthusiasm by her audience. We were entertained at dinner aboard a luxurious Israeli liner and, in the light of the setting sun, I had a beautiful view of Haifa, so modern and prosperous despite the recent war. On the last evening the delegates were entertained at a folk festival in the municipal stadium and Ben Gurion, the octogenarian Prime Minister, spoke with a spirit and eloquence that many young men might have envied. Despite these festivities, we were reminded of the difficult situation of the time whenever we saw the Israeli soldiers on sentry duty at the doors of our hotels. For all the apparent calm and quiet, the danger of armed conflict was always present.

A few years later, Mrs. Golda Meir, now the Israeli Prime Minister, invited me to represent Canada at a congress in Jerusalem that had as its theme the role of women in reconstruction and peace. There were eight official languages, and the delegates, all strong and brilliant speakers, easily held the attention of the audience. The sessions lasted from 8:30 in the morning till five o'clock in the afternoon, with scarcely an hour for lunch. Needless to say, such prolonged meetings were not followed by social gatherings. I was the only Canadian delegate, probably because, as well as being a member of the Voice of Women, I was bilingual. There were two delegates from the United States, a white woman representing the thousands of members of American women's clubs and a black woman from Philadelphia, a journalist at the United Nations; their excellent papers attracted much attention and were highly praised.

On my way home, I stopped off in Paris, where a meeting of NATO was in session, to join a group of women from NATO Women's Peace Force. We wanted to present a petition to the committee of the defence ministers of NATO opposing the proliferation of nuclear weapons, and decided to go to the organization's headquarters at about one o'clock in the afternoon, hoping to meet with either the Secretary General, Monteo Brasio, or the representatives of our respective countries. Just as we were about to show our credentials we were informed that only one of us would be admitted. Our leader Mrs. Clark, an American, felt that there should be at least two in the delegation and, as she did not speak French and wanted a bilingual witness at her side, she chose me to accompany her. Everyone agreed to this proposal. These preparations proved futile, however, for a few minutes later, to our amazement, a paddy wagon drew up and we were forced unresisting to get in and be carried off to jail. Our "weapons"—that is, our mirrors and nail-files—were removed from our purses; each of us was interrogated separately and then we were locked in a cell without heat, water, or food. We passed the time singing and writing reports. At about five-thirty we were released with the warning that all assembly at NATO headquarters was prohibited and that at the next offence we would be expelled from the country and forbidden to return. That evening almost two thousand delegates gathered in the *Salle de la Mutualité* to give an account of their experiences. Jean Rostand, the famous biologist, gave a very cutting speech, and flowers were presented to all those who had been imprisoned. I was chosen to be official interpreter—an honour that once again reflected credit on Canada. The delegates returned home more conscious than ever before of the enormity of their task.

During the years that followed we prepared and submitted a great many briefs advocating various social reforms. Before the Royal Commission on Bilingualism and Biculturalism we established our position thus: The French and English cultures had the right to survive in Canada and any division could only lead to our destruction.

That same year, Voice of Women of Quebec prepared a document that was supported by Voice of Women of Canada and signed by Ghislaine Laurendeau, Simone Chartrand, Marthe Legault, Elizabeth Rossinger, Marcelle Vanasse, Ann Gertler, and myself. In the hope that it would be given to one of the commissions at the Ecumenical Council, Vatican II, copies were sent to Their Eminences Cardinals Roy, Léger, and Flahiff, as well as to a number of Canadian bishops who were going to Rome. The chief points covered by our submission were as follows: 1. condemnation of war; 2. condemnation of atomic and thermonuclear war; 3. peace agencies; 4. general disarmament, negotiations, and condemnation of limited wars; 5. doctrine of non-violence and conscientious objection; 6. responsibilities of individuals, families, and schools in establishing peace. There was a commission on war at the Council but we have never been told whether our brief was presented to it. However, the day after the discussion of the draft dealing with the problems of peace, Le Devoir reported the following words from a statement by Cardinal Léger: "War must be explicitly condemned in all its forms. It is no longer possible to make any distinction between a just and an unjust war."[9]

In July, 1964, I represented Voice of Women at the World Peace Congress in Helsinki. The People's Republic of China, the USSR, the United States, Argentina, Brazil, Chile, India, North Vietnam, and a great many other countries sent delegations. Of fifteen hundred delegates, about three hundred were women. Among the observers there were some forty Catholic priests as well as a number of Greek Orthodox bishops and Protestant clergymen.

The Vietnamese were the stars of the congress, for everyone felt great sympathy for this country that had been torn apart by war for more than twenty-five years. I was elected to the steering committee of about a hundred delegates that prepared the agenda for the deliberations. At the meeting we adopted a resolution proposed by Jean-Paul Sartre, condemning the United States for intervention in Vietnam. Here, then, was a new example of what Voice of Women was doing, breaking all boundaries to reach people of every ideology, race, and culture in their search for points of agreement and cooperation. It was obvious to us that every assembly that brought together capitalists, communists, anarchists, and the uncommitted was of value.

In the autumn of 1965, a delegation from Voice of Women went to Russia at the invitation of the Committee of Soviet Women. This delegation was made up of Martha Friesen of Vancouver, whose husband was a professor at the University of British Columbia, Brigitte Brigden of Winnipeg, and Nancy Pocock of Toronto, Jeanne Duval of Montreal, former vice-president of the *Confédération des syndicats nationaux,* and myself. An Air Canada plane took us to Brussels, where we boarded a Sabena flight to Moscow. On our arrival in the Soviet capital, we found a huge crowd waiting, flowers in hand. It was pleasant, for once, to be considered important but this seemed a little excessive. At that moment, the arrival of an Aeroflot flight from Paris with Yuri Gagarin on board explained our error; the flowers and the welcome were for him. As soon as he stepped from the plane, his wife rushed to embrace him, leaving on the hero's cheek, to our astonishment, the clear imprint of her kiss. We thought ruefully of all the tubes of lipstick we had brought for the Russian women, not knowing that East Germany provided all they wanted.

While in Moscow, we visited the Kremlin and admired the treasures of the tsars—the innumerable precious stones that adorned the dresses of the tsarinas, the icons, the priestly vestments, the swords and daggers with their chased handles, and even the saddles of the horses, the solid gold dishes, and a great many other marvels that transported us into an unreal world. Visitors were asked to remove their shoes and wear the slippers provided, so as not to damage the floors of the palace.

After visiting the modest house where Lenin lived we went to Red Square, where our status as foreigners permitted us to break into the uninterrupted file of people waiting to see the body of the father of the revolution lying in its open casket. Behind his mausoleum are the tombs of other illustrious figures of the revolution. Stalin's tomb, however, had been removed and the memory of this man who once caused the great and powerful of this earth to tremble seemed deliberately consigned to oblivion. Standing beside Lenin's remains, I was reminded of my meeting in Paris some years before with an old French socialist who had known Lenin well when he lived in exile in France. This gentleman told us about the debate between those who wanted to improve conditions for the Russians by negotiations and those who maintained that only violence could attain the desired results. Lenin opted for violence and returned to Russia with his companions, where he led the bloody revolution that resulted in the régime we know today.

Leningrad—formerly St. Petersburg—is surely one of the most beautiful cities in the world. It was built by Peter the Great, who was inspired by the cities he had admired in France. Hundreds of bridges span the Neva River, which flows through the city, its banks lined with beautiful buildings. At the Hermitage Museum, extraordinary *objets d'art* are on display, as well as the works of world-renowned painters and a marvellous collection of jewels of all sorts. We were told that during the war, when the Germans had spent whole months at the gates, the people defended the city street by street and house by house. The roof of the Hermitage was camouflaged with greenery and branches, and all the works of art were carefully wrapped and buried in the ground. Another part of the city that particularly impressed us was the cemetery where six hundred and fifty thousand men and women, the valiant defenders of Leningrad against repeated attacks of the Germans, are buried. At the entrance, an account of this heroic resistance is engraved on a stone arch and a loudspeaker emits music that is like a constant lament. At the end of an avenue edged with blood-red roses stands a statue about six feet high of a mother holding her dead child in her arms. On either side of her, water falls from fountains drop by drop, like tears, and for as far as the eye can see are rows of little tombstones, each bearing a single inscription: *1944*, the year of the siege.

On the outskirts of Leningrad, in a magnificent garden, stands a retirement home for elderly artists. Here we met a woman who had sung with Chaliapin. Another, who had danced with Pavlova, had spent some time in Switzerland and France and was delighted to be able to talk to me in French. I asked her why she had not accompanied Pavlova on her American tour, and she replied that she had not wanted to leave her beloved country. Pasternak had said the same sort of thing and this only confirmed my belief that love of country is particularly deep among the Russians.

The Committee of Soviet Women had provided us with two guides. One of them was a pretty woman of about thirty-two, a graduate in political economy, who spoke English and French fluently. She had spent two years in New York and had been, she said, struck by the strong attachment of the Americans to material things. She was the only one in her family who held a card in the Communist party and explained to us that out of two hundred and fifty million Russians only about ten million are active members of the party. "Far more is demanded of us than of the others," she told me, and went on, "Madame, I am an atheist and a Communist whereas you are a capitalist and a Catholic. Yet one thing unites us: we want peace. We both have children and we don't want them to be killed stupidly in a senseless war. We must negotiate so that it will never again be necessary to fight to resolve a problem."

Our other guide was a very slender woman who spoke exquisite French and in her youth had had a French teacher. Our clothes fascinated her and I remember her asking my permission one day to copy a black velvet dress and coral-pink coat I was wearing. GUM, which was the big store in Moscow, offered garments which were poorly cut and badly put together. As a result, people of more discriminating tastes preferred to make their own clothes.

When we left Leningrad, we were able to go to Baku, in the southern province of Azerbaidjan, famous for its oil-wells. The local committee of Soviet women came to meet us, among them an ophthalmologist of international renown and the provincial Minister of Social Welfare, who had won fame as a pilot during

World War II. These pleasant guides showed us around the town, which extends on pilings for several miles into the sea. The workers who come to burrow into the depths of the ocean for oil live in temporary shelters during the week, only going home on Saturdays. At our request, we were taken to see a steel-mill where working conditions seemed much less favourable than at home.

After Baku came Sochi, a well-known resort on the Black Sea, where workers come for a rest during their vacations. Beautiful buildings are at the disposal of the various unions for their members. Our hotel was beside the sea and, though the suite I occupied included a living room, bedroom, and bathroom, the last-mentioned had a basin without a plug and a toilet without a seat. As there was no glass in the windows of the hotel dining room, birds fluttered constantly over our heads.

One evening in Moscow, Olga Chetchetkina, a member of the editorial staff of *Pravda*, invited me to her office, which was not far from our hotel, the Soviet Skaia. Four thousand people work in the immense Pravda building and there are also two hundred and fifty reporters scattered about the world. The daily circulation of the paper is roughly six million copies. After showing me around the offices and the presses, Mrs. Chekchetkina introduced me to the assistant editor, who presented me with a bronze medal bearing the figure of Lenin. Mrs. Chetchetkina speaks English, French, Italian, and German, as well as her mother tongue, and has come to Canada on three occasions to attend congresses of the Voice of Women. She told me that one day, like many other Soviet women, she had chosen to renounce all female coquetry in order to dedicate herself to her country.

After this visit to the USSR, I went to Geneva to attend a meeting, chaired by Lord Attlee, to discuss the organization of a world parliament. I then returned to Canada, to continue my work for peace, more aware than ever before of the importance of this cause.

XV

Where There's a Will, There's a Way

In October, 1966, I attended an international seminar in Rome on the participation of women in public life. Delegates, observers, and guests from thirty countries represented more than fifty organizations devoted to the advancement of women. The meetings were chaired by Dr. Teresita Sandeschi Scelba, president of the National Council of Italian women. Mrs. Marguerite Thibert, Doctor of Letters and former head of the women and young people's division of the International Labour Office, attended as a recorder. A great many briefs were presented, dealing with, among other things, the participation of women in municipal affairs, in public offices, in the judiciary, in legislative bodies and governments, as well as with the role of women in the economy, in the social services, and in the news media. After four days of deliberation, recommendations were drawn up to be submitted to the United Nations, to national authorities, and to all the associations devoted to the betterment of human life; the congress urged the organizations represented to act together and without delay to exert pressure upon the various governments.

As I listened to these discussions, I was carried back to another meeting – that of the International Council of Women held in Paris around 1938 under the chairmanship of Mrs. Joliot Curie, at which I had heard debates on exactly the same subjects. A quarter of a century later, women had progressed very little and were still at the discussion stage. Mrs. Fernand Simard, the president of Voice of Women of Quebec, had accompanied me to the congress and we both deplored all these fiery statements that produced so little. Yet, we felt, there would have been a much more logical way to proceed. As a matter of fact, women seemed to be in retreat all over the world. In France immediately after the war, there were some forty women members of the National Assembly, whereas now there were only four or five. It seems that when women fight beside their men for freedom, they are better integrated and have less time to be distracted or monopolized by matters of secondary importance. But strange to say, once the wars are over and peace restored, they return to their homes and are far less interested in social problems. Of course it is normal for domestic tasks to absorb a large part of their energies, but is that any reason to refuse to work in the public sector? Generally speaking, women are less accepted in positions of command. It would be hard to imagine a woman head of government in Canada or the United States, for instance, though, in the Third World, several women have attained the highest offices: Indira Gandhi in India, Golda Meir in Israel, and Sirimajo Bandaranaike in Ceylon. In any event, especially in the West, there is little cooperation between the sexes and I admit that it is often the women themselves who set up obstacles in their own way. In my speech at the end of the Rome sessions, I expressed the hope that, in future congresses, men and women would work together for the common good. In a democracy, all the citizens are governed by the same laws but these are generally drawn up and enacted by men. If society is to be improved, a greater number of competent women must make their presence felt in all spheres of life, politics included.

From the very beginning of my involvement in social questions, I saw the urgent need for positive and practical action. While still quite young, I was asked to be a member of the Commission on Minimum Wages. I discovered then, with sorrow, the lamentable economic position of our female labour force. Women worked a ten-hour day for very low wages and some profiteers even hired teenaged girls during the summer for trifling sums. Another neglected group was the rural women school-teachers. One of them, a woman of about thirty, submitted her case to the *Ligue des Droits de la Femme*, begging us to help her. She taught in a country school where her pupils ranged from the first to the eighth grade. At six o'clock every morning, she had to light the fire so that the classroom would be warm enough when the children arrived at about half past eight. Her salary of a hundred and fifty dollars a year forced her to eat very meagrely and sometimes do without food altogether. Two years later, this unfortunate young woman was dying of tuberculosis, obviously the victim of these inhuman working conditions. The authorities responsible for the organization and development of education in Quebec showed very little concern for this section of our social élite. The following is a testimony of the time:

Working-Conditions of Rural Women Teachers
(1936-1962)

I have never been able to understand why our French-Canadian farmer, who is otherwise very intelligent, does not hesitate for a moment to lay out three or even four dollars a month to get his horses shod and yet refuses to pay–if I allow twenty free-holders per school-district–the sum of one dollar a month to have his five or six children shod for the needs of life. What I can understand even less is that it should be considered very natural (as it is) that our governors–those who are presumed to think for those who do not think for themselves–should pay agronomists very well to oversee the rearing of pigs and lambs and yet have waited till this year to think of raising the salaries of those men and women who are dying of starvation while they devote themselves to the education of the race.[1]

A manifesto published under the auspices of the *Association des institutrices rurales de la province de Québec* includes the following:

She (the teacher) makes an annual contribution of three percent of her income to the primary teacher's retirement fund .... If after laboriously and stoically completing her twenty-five years' teaching, she expresses the wish to retire and obtain her pension, she is obliged to provide certificate after certificate and sent from one doctor to another. A certificate of "broken in health by teaching" is not sufficient; the verdict has to be "killed by teaching." When the thousand formalities have been completed, she wins her case and is offered a mouthful of bread and a bone to gnaw–one hundred and fifty dollars a year, an insulting and insufficient pension.[2]

In view of such a state of affairs, a woman of superior intelligence and indomitable energy decided to form a union to protect those who were sacrificing themselves to the education of our children. This was Miss Laure Gaudreault, a teacher in a rural school in La Malbaie. In 1936, she founded the first *Union des institutrices rurales catholiques* in Clermont in Charlevoix county. As my husband represented this district in Parliament, I had the opportunity to meet her and work with her. I have always felt great affection for this admirable woman and at the celebration of the twenty-fifth anniversary of the granting of the women's provincial vote she was one of the guests of honour of the *Ligue*.

As I mentioned in a previous chapter, the *Ligue des Droits de la Femme* was originally founded to obtain the provincial vote. Since women had to be enfranchised on all levels at once, the *Ligue* simultaneously undertook a number of struggles it considered essential: the admission of women to the liberal professions, their right to vote in cooperatives, and their eligibility for jury duty. Although a few reforms in the Civil Code were obtained in 1931, the *Ligue* considered these far from sufficient. As a result, a new committee was formed in 1944 to work more intensely for the revision of certain statutes. Two eminent attorneys, Jacques Perreault and Elizabeth Monk, joined us and submitted important briefs to the Committee for the Revision of the Civil Code. As the commission was composed of two male members—Senator Léon Methot of Trois-Rivières, the chairman, and Mr. Léon Balcer, the secretary—I had approached Prime Minister Duplessis in an effort to have a qualified woman included. Such a request, needless to say, was not granted. Several years later a new *commission des droits civils* was appointed under the chairmanship of the Honourable Thibaudeault Rinfret, former Chief Justice of the Supreme Court of Canada. Ironically he was seconded by Senator Jean-François Pouliot, whose anti-feminist opinions were widely known. As a result, the desired amendments were prepared with disheartening slowness.

Although Bill 16, which was passed in 1964 following the report of this commission, improved the status of married women, especially those who were married separate as to property, nevertheless the law retained the principle of the community of property which was, therefore, under the husband's control. In the middle of the twentieth century this was somewhat anachronistic. Curiously enough, our lawmakers are still seeking inspiration from what is done in Europe or elsewhere instead of having the courage to innovate and legislate not with reference to the past but with a view to the future.

175

A few years later, in 1969, a new law was passed dealing with married couples and their property. The principle of community of property no longer applied to inherited property. While this marked new progress in the status of married women, it also gave rise to tremendous complications which will probably cause couples simply to have a contract drawn up at the time of their marriage establishing their respective rights over their possessions.

While my husband was a member of the House of Commons, I was asked to accept the vice presidency of the French section of the Canadian Adult Education Association. I thus had the opportunity to meet such eminent educators as Father Moses M. Coady, who organized cooperatives among the fishermen of the Maritimes. At this time, Mr. George Bouchard, a Liberal member of parliament who later became Deputy Minister of Agriculture in Ottawa, was president of the French section of the Association, in which Colonel Wilfrid Bovey of McGill was also active. It was becoming urgent to form a Quebec branch, which was done. I served as its president for several years but when Duplessis returned to power, I thought it advisable to resign and yield place to someone whose name, shall we say, would not be tainted with federalism or liberalism. The work of this association still continues and adult education now absorbs a large segment of our public teaching.

In 1967 I founded the *Fédération des femmes du Québec* to coordinate the efforts of various women's organizations and thus make them more effective. Rather than found a new association, I would have preferred to work with some already existing group, such as the *Fédération nationale Saint-Jean-Baptiste*. I therefore met with the leaders of this organization and asked them to modernize their rules and their constitution, which dated from 1910. For instance, they were determined at all costs to have a chaplain, for which I saw no reason since we were all Christians and Catholic women, fully aware of our duties. But Louis Hémon wrote in *Maria Chapdelaine:* "In Quebec nothing must change." I quickly saw that this and other differences in our views created insurmountable barriers.

The first president of the new *Fédération des femmes du Québec* was Mrs. Rejane Laberge-Cola, a lawyer who subsequently became the first woman appointed a Superior Court judge. Then came

Mrs. Rita Cadieux, a graduate of the *Université de Montréal* and a member of the Canadian delegation to the United Nations. Mrs. Marie-Paule Dandois of Quebec City succeeded her and the federation is now headed by Mrs. Yvette Rousseau of Sherbrooke, a former vice-president of the *Confédération des Syndicats nationaux*. In our new Quebec federation there is no discrimination as to race, colour, or religion, and everyone is welcome.

All women should be involved with matters of health and education. But before this can be possible, there must be increased opportunities for them to obtain the knowledge required in the areas of economics, political science, and administrative matters that will enable them to attack problems of greater scope and vital importance to the community. Since we are governed by laws, we must attempt to amend them whenever necessary, for the greatest good of society. Changes are being made here and there–but very, very slowly.

A typical case is that of the Montreal Catholic School Board to which no woman had ever been appointed up to 1970. In fact, a law stipulated that to be a school commissioner, one had to be the father of a family. To change this, I formed an emergency committee of six people. The committee received an immediate response from the Minister of Education, Mr. Jean-Guy Cardinal, and also from the Leader of the Opposition, Mr. Jean Lesage, but none at all from Mr. René Lévesque, the leader of the *Parti québécois*. A telephone call from the Prime Minister, Mr. Jean-Jacques Bertrand, informed us that he was in complete agreement with our cause and the necessary amendment to permit women to become school commissioners would be passed at once. This was done and a few days later the archdiocese appointed Mrs. Thérèse Lavoie-Roux, an eminently qualified woman, to the Catholic School Board. She is now chairman of the Montreal School Commission.

When Bill 63, the school language bill, was introduced in the Quebec Legislative Assembly in the autumn of 1969, there were huge demonstrations by teachers and students. I immediately telephoned the various women's associations asking them to protest publicly against the participation of children in disputes of this sort. Whether one was for or against Bill 63 was not the point.

It was simply a matter of taking the necessary steps to prevent children from being drawn into a problem they were too young to judge. I was unable to obtain any cooperation from the associations I contacted, and my efforts were in vain.

On the 31st of May, 1968, I had the honour to receive a doctorate *honoris causa* from Mr. Justice Lucien Tremblay, Chancellor of the *Université de Montréal*. In his presentation address, Mr. Philippe Garrigues, Dean of the Faculty of Social Sciences, spoke of my efforts to improve the conditions of women, the family, and the population as a whole over the past thirty years. A great many people came to the convocation and I received many congratulations. At that time, student demonstrations were becoming increasingly importunate and I took this opportunity to suggest to the university authorities that they should arrange to have a television program—on the CBC or a private station—which could be called, "This is the university speaking." I believe that if the various institutions concerned had been able to work together, the program would have been very useful; parents and students could have exchanged views with the university administrators and obtained answers to their questions. I already had a daily program called "Voice of Women," on which I endeavoured to answer all the questions of my viewers. To judge by the response I received, the program helped many people. All subjects were treated seriously. As I have always been involved with social questions, life has taught me a great deal. Is there any better school than that of the fire of action?

Some twenty-five years earlier, long before television, and when even radio was still new, my regular program, *Fémina*, had tried to inform the public on various important questions and the need for amendments to our Civil Code. Only by using all the means at my disposal was I able to render some service to the women of my country and induce others to work with me. Together we have accomplished some essential tasks, but many very urgent ones remain and "the labourers are few." I cannot stress too often how important it is in all fields of endeavour to band together and coordinate all efforts to ensure better planning. That is why I worked with such dedication for the *Société des concerts symphoniques de Montréal*, which was founded in November 1934. Unfortunately the work was once again made more difficult by the lack of mutual understanding that so often arises between people who ought to be able to forget their own ambitions and work for the common good. With this same objective, I helped to found the *Fédération des oeuvres de charité canadiennes-françaises.*

Another difficulty that constantly hindered coordinating the various movements was the division of which Hugh MacLennan speaks in *Two Solitudes*. This unfortunate division between the two ethnic groups goes a long way to explain the separatist movement, which has existed in a latent form for several generations. The economic differences between English and French-speaking Canadians in our province and the lack of contact between them are other factors that have separated us until now. Here as elsewhere I made an attempt to establish harmony at the time of our struggle to obtain the women's vote.

During the 1930s, the Young Business Women of Toronto invited me to speak to them about our work. Some years after this, my first public address outside Quebec, I was invited by the Association of Canadian Clubs to give a series of addresses throughout Canada. From 1956 to 1962, I crossed the whole country, explaining the reasons for the dissatisfaction of increasing numbers of Quebeckers with the treatment we received from so many English-speaking Canadians. Whether it was Hamilton, Winnipeg, Vancouver, or Saint John, I noticed the same curiosity everywhere about the events taking place in Quebec. I admitted that we were certainly not without sin but suggested that, before condemning us, the rest of Canada should first examine its own conscience. I used to cite an incident of the last war when a French Canadian officer in the Canadian army, stationed in northern British Columbia to guard our coast against possible attack from the Japanese, called his wife in Montreal to wish her Merry Christmas. Suddenly he was interrupted by the operator, who pointed out that since the country was at war, "foreign languages" were not permitted and he must speak English. I need not describe the officer's indignation.

One of the most famous wartime civil rights cases was that of Mr. Roncarelli, a Montreal restaurant owner and member of the Jehovah's Witnesses, whose liquor license was revoked and wines confiscated after he had paid the fine for some others of his sect who had been arrested for actions judged illegal at that time. He approached a Civil Liberties Committee to which I belonged and our group organized a big rally in the National Monument to protest this arbitrary action of the Duplessis government. Hundreds of people attended. Mr. Roncarelli then asked his lawyer, Mr. A. L. Stein, whether he could obtain compensation from the provincial government. After thoroughly examining the matter, it was decided to bring a personal suit against Maurice Duplessis; Mr. Frank Scott, lawyer and professor, agreed to take the case. It lasted for thirteen years and finally a Supreme Court judgment found Duplessis guilty and required him to pay Mr. Roncarelli fifty thousand dollars' damages. After this judgment a great many friends and admirers gathered spontaneously at Mr. Scott's house to congratulate him.

I have already mentioned the work of the various Japanese-Canadian committees during the last war. It was with a view to other possible injustices of this sort that a handful of concerned Canadians decided to join together to safeguard the inherent rights of all our citizens. In 1960, such well-known people as Pierre Elliott Trudeau, Gérard Pelletier, Jean Marchand, Frank Scott, and many others who were interested in defending the rights of Canadian citizens and especially those citizens who lived in Quebec decided to found the League for Human Rights. Mr. Alban Flamand was the first chairman. Through the years René Hurtubise, Claude Armand Shepherd, Professor Claude Forget, and myself have succeeded to the presidency. The league now has a federal charter, and the publisher Jacques Hébert is its chairman. The association has presented a number of briefs to the Commission for the Revision of the Civil Code, dealing in turn with the legal status of women, the child adoption law, and the divorce law; it has been involved in such problems as obscene literature, the oath of allegiance required of new Canadians, and various other questions of principle directly concerned with human rights. It has endeavoured to improve conditions in our prisons and penitentiaries and has been particularly concerned about the frequent prison suicides of recent years. In 1967, the year designated by the United Nations for the celebration of human rights, committees were formed in all parts of Canada and our Quebec members were very active.

When Claude Wagner was Minister of Justice in the Lesage government, he set up the Consultative Committee on the Administration of Justice to study different laws and make recommendations to the government. Its members, who were chosen from various milieus, were twenty in number and met approximately every two months. The first chairman was Jean Martineau, then the head of the Canada Council. I was vice chairman and Louis Marceau was secretary. The latter is now ombudsman for the Province of Quebec. Of all the members of the committee only the secretary received a salary. Legislation dealing with coroners, police organization, the ombudsman, and legal aid were submitted to us. This committee is still active.

Moved by the tragic situation in Vietnam, where war has been raging for more than twenty-five years, Dr. Lloyd Williams, a McGill professor and a Quaker, decided to found an association to provide badly needed medical assistance to civilians in both North and South Vietnam. I became president of the association, which took the name Quebec Medical Aid for Vietnam. About twelve thousand dollars in contributions poured in from all corners of the province. One day a wealthy American visitor to *Man and His World* came to see me with her son to make a gift to our committee. I was, of course, expecting a fairly subsantial donation but I gasped when she handed me two thousand dollars in American bills, refusing even a receipt. She asked whether we would accept further contributions that she hoped to send us. Needless to say, my reply was in the affirmative.

Throughout my work I have always had the help and support of the Jewish community–in the CCF, in Voice of Women, and during my long struggle to obtain the provincial vote. The fact that this community is itself a minority and often persecuted, has made solid bonds between us. When Mrs. Golda Meir organized a congress in Jerusalem on reconstruction and peace, I was invited by the Israeli consul general to go to the Near East for the meetings; I was the only representative of Canada. During Expo 67, the National Council of Jewish Women of Canada awarded me its medal as the "woman of the century" of Quebec for "my significant contribution to the general well-being, on the occasion of the centenary." The medal was presented to me at a luncheon given by the organization in June, 1967. That same year the *Société de Criminologie du Québec* also awarded me a medal as "the person who has been most distinguished in the defence of human rights and the ideals of justice in our society." As chairman of the League for Human Rights, I had worked actively to bring about amendments to our Civil Code and to alleviate the dreadful living conditions in our prisons and penitentiaries. Then, on the 6th of July of that year, I received the "medal for distinguished service of the Order of Canada."

At the end of World War II, I had been made a member of the Order of the British Empire for my work with the Wartime Prices and Trade Board. My experience with consumers during the war had made me aware of another worthy cause, that of the plight of the consumer, who is now more exploited than ever before and bears almost the entire weight of the rise in the cost of living. In May, 1969, I became president of the Canadian Consumers Association for Quebec. I was very anxious to resume this work since I had noticed that the national organization we had founded during the war had over the years been supported in Quebec chiefly by the English-speaking population. Since then, excellent publicity and a generous donation from a Canadian foundation have enabled us to enlarge our ranks and set up new groups. As the result of pressure from our organization across the country, we now have a Minister for Consumer Affairs in Ottawa and most of the provinces have similar ministries.

XVI

Tomorrow Is Another Day

While I was in the midst of all these activities, I was startled one evening in September 1970 to receive a telephone call from the Prime Minister of Canada, the Right Honourable Pierre Elliott Trudeau, offering me a seat in the Senate. I could have no delusions about the time I would occupy this position, for a law passed in 1965 obliged senators to retire when they reached the age of seventy-five. Even so, since I believed the position would give me greater facility to work for my country, I accepted, with the intention of sitting as an independent, free of all political attachment. I stress this point since my confrères in the CCF and later in the NDP have always refused to sit in the Upper House as long as the much-needed reforms of the Senate remained to be carried out. I chose to represent the vacancy of Mille-Îles as my father came from Terrebonne, a town in that region.

On the 8th of October, I went to Ottawa for the opening of Parliament and was sworn in as a senator. Deeply moved, I was carried back to the now distant past when my husband, as Speaker of the House of Commons and then a minister in the King cabinet, had played such an important role in the government of the day. I had never even imagined that some thirty years later I would occupy a seat in the Upper House, where I would have the advantage of speaking to a very much wider and more representative audience about the things that have always been close to my heart.

The session was barely underway when Canada and the world learned with amazement of the successive kidnappings of Mr. James Cross, the British Trade Commissioner in Montreal, and Mr. Pierre Laporte, the Quebec Minister of Labour. Difficult days passed and then came the horrifying news of Mr. Laporte's murder. The country was plunged into tragedy. The Prime Minister of Quebec, Mr. Robert Bourassa, had already asked the Canadian Prime Minister to proclaim the War Measures Act. There were rumours that the Quebec government was to be replaced by a so-called parallel government and some of the news media even named those who would be part of it. I personally still feel that these rumours had a solid basis. The people named were only too ready to believe that they were in possession of the truth and considered themselves the saviours of Quebec. Yet they had no mandate from the people. Once again I observed the lack of any spirit of democracy in my province.

Along with thousands of my fellow Canadians, I shall never forget the impressive speech of the Honourable Pierre Elliot Trudeau on the night of the 16th of October in which he announced with great calm and firmness that he must unfortunately put the War Measures Act into force. The army had been sent to guard strategic and public places. The behaviour of our soldiers was irreproachable and their presence did a great deal to reassure the population. If the War Measures Act, whose imposition has been so violently criticized by some people, had been applied with strictness, a number of radio stations would certainly not have been able to pass on the messages from the FLQ, most of which were found in trash-cans. In Ottawa, the army protected the officials, senators, members of parliament, and judges, and guarded the safety of the members of the diplomatic corps. In my inaugural speech, I expressed my entire approval of the government's courageous action in proclaiming the War Measures Act.

Despite these tragic events, the government was continuing to work in the international field and I was very pleased to be able to congratulate the authorities for having finally established diplomatic relations with the People's Republic of China. As a member of the CCF and Voice of Women, I remembered how insistently these organizations had urged the governments of the day to grant this recognition. At the time of Expo 67, Voice of Women had even passed a resolution asking the commissioner of the exposition, Mr. Pierre Dupuy, to obtain the participation of the People's Republic of China. He had replied that, though he was personally sympathetic to our request, the absence of diplomatic relations between the two countries made this impossible. So my regrets of 1967 had now changed to joy. There can be no doubt that the presence of a Chinese ambassador in Ottawa will enable Canadians to know more about what is happening in that distant country. We will also become increasingly aware of a way of thinking different from our own, which in the long run can have only beneficial results.

As I concluded my inaugural speech, I could not help referring to the economic problems of my province. I therefore protested vigorously against certain agricultural controls which were likely to balkanize the country and encourage black market activity. The creation of FEDCO (*Fédération des producteurs d'oeufs de consommation du Québec*), which received permission from the Quebec Marketing Board to control the price of eggs, is an unfortunate example. This legislation caused serious difficulties between the provinces and led to the "chicken and egg war." Not only are eggs now more expensive in Quebec than in Ontario or Manitoba, but the province has paid more than two million dollars to FEDCO—money from our taxes—and black market activity is widespread. Once again we can see Quebec suffering from its own lack of forethought.

A little later, though I was fully aware that the administration of justice is a provincial matter, I drew the senators' attention to the fact that, in Quebec, women were not eligible to serve on juries—a right they possessed in all other provinces except Newfoundland. To my great satisfaction a bill was introduced in Newfoundland a few weeks later, putting an end to this discrimination; Quebec followed suit in May 1971. Many years before, while I was president of the *Ligue des Droits de la Femme*, we had included the right of women to serve on juries among our objectives. This was considered very daring and came to nothing.

In February, I dealt with the report of the Royal Commission on the Status of Women, which had been tabled in the Upper House on the 8th of December, 1970. At that moment, a certain point struck me: the fight to improve the status of women now dated back ninety years; they had been voting for more than fifty-five years, and yet they had never represented more than one percent of the total elected members of our legislatures. The facts in the report dealing with the various aspects of Canadian life are all the more disturbing since they are the results of objective

185

and non-ideological analysis. They only confirm what everyone has long known about the discrimination that women face.

The very spirit of the report aims to bring down the wall of prejudice between the sexes and remove the barriers that society has erected between men and women. But although the trade unions and a great many other associations, as well as private individuals, have endorsed the general principles of this study, its recommendations have remained dead letters to all intents and purposes; no practical proposals have been put forward. Grace MacInnis, my long-time friend and the only woman member of the House of Commons, was, like many others, of the opinion that a single member of the cabinet should be designated to deal with the recommendations of the report. I, on the contrary, thought that each minister should fulfil his responsibilities in this field and see to the implementation of the resolutions of particular concern to his department. My view did not prevail and the task was entrusted to the Honourable Robert Andras, the Secretary of State for Urban Affairs.

As I was still deeply concerned with the problems of Vietnam, I seized this opportunity to ask the government leader in the Senate, the Honourable Paul Martin, whether our government had made representations to the United States about the use of defoliants as part of American military strategy in Vietnam and, particularly, whether napalm and its ingredients are manufactured in Canada. It seems that the answer to both questions is no, but since business and industry in the United States and Canada are so inter-connected it is difficult to determine precisely whether or not napalm or its constituent elements are produced here. One may, therefore, wonder whether some Canadian products have not been used indirectly for American ends with which we do not agree.

At the end of May, I supported Bill S-17, which was introduced by Senator Benidickson to amend the Competition Act to include banking. The banks had just raised their service charge to twenty cents per cheque. They charged about eleven per cent interest on loans while offering only four and a half per cent on deposits. Borrowing, which is encouraged by a great spate of advertising, enables the banks to multiply their profits with our money. In 1970, they made $529,000,000 profit and the dividend to shareholders rose to eleven per cent. That was why I supported Senator Benidickson's bill, hoping to benefit the consumer. One may wonder why the press did not give more space to this question. Several newspapers, even among the most respected, prefer to make a great hue and cry about the scandals of the moment. They rarely give enough publicity to more serious issues, in order to educate the public and, by the same token, help get laws passed for the greater good of society. Unless the news is devoted to essential questions rather than trivialities, it is hard for citizens to exert sufficient pressure to get action from the authorities.

As a member of the joint Senate-Commons Committee on the Constitution, I travelled to several cities across Canada to meet the public, "probe hearts and minds," and try to determine how best to amend or repatriate the British North America Act. Since simultaneous translation was obligatory, no one could use incomprehension of the language as an excuse for failure to express an opinion. The committee was generally well received but there were occasions when discussion was difficult and, indeed, at times impossible. In Montreal and Sherbrooke, for instance, some people refused even to consider the question. They had come to the sittings with the clear intention of creating disturbances and preventing anyone from expressing an opinion contrary to their own. This sort of attitude has always surprised me. I have so often heard the Fathers of Confederation blamed for shutting themselves up in a room in Charlottetown and drafting the BNA Act on their own. And now in many places, despite this opportunity to discuss the matter and suggest whatever changes seem advisable, people throw the room into an uproar and speak on quite unrelated subjects. How regrettable I found this negative attitude of a large number of our citizens, who seemed not to understand the meaning of democracy. The phrase participatory democracy is on everyone's lips, but few put it into practice.

I was able to attend sittings of various other committees, such as those dealing with foreign affairs, poverty, commerce and banking, and the mass media. I made a statement in the Senate one day about the sale of an Ontario publishing house to American interests, recalling that by a similar transaction several years before one of our largest Quebec publishing houses had passed into foreign hands. Far be it from me to restrict the publication of the books we read to our own country; however, I think it would be extremely dangerous to remove all Canadian initiative from such a field.

The government asked me, in my capacity as senator, to head the France-Canada delegation to a congress in Marseilles. When the sessions were over, our consul, Mr. Eugène Bussières, entertained us in his magnificent apartment situated on the heights of the city with a splendid view of the Mediterranean and the surrounding mountains. This reception made an unforgettable impression on us all. After the congress, the delegates went their separate ways–to Corsica or Paris or some other city in France. In my case, an unfortunate mishap prevented my going to Paris before I returned to Canada. I would like to have gone there to judge for myself a recent incident when the Quebec Minister of Education was treated in a cavalier fashion by our students, all of whom were studying abroad at the tax-payers' expense. I would have been interested in ascertaining on the spot whether the brain-washing there is the same as is practised here in Quebec.

It would be hard for me to mention all the activities in which I participated during my brief nine-month sojourn in the Senate. Contrary to popular belief, being a senator is not a sinecure for anyone who really wants to make full use of a unique opportunity to work for the betterment of our country. A great many studies are continually underway in various committees and supply the two houses with useful information for the promulgation of laws as well as all other sorts of mutual assistance. As soon as I arrived in my office at nine in the morning, I always hastened to open my mail and answer it at once, which left me free to attend the committee meetings. In the afternoons and evenings the Senate sittings filled all my time. I took advantage of every chance that arose to meet with members of parliament and senators to discuss various problems of public interest. "When ideas collide, light results," goes an old saying that still retains all its sense.

On the 30th of June, 1971, the session adjourned for the summer recess and on the 10th of July, I reached the fateful age that forced me to retire from the Senate. So another period in my life had just come to an end. Now that I possessed an experience and a maturity that only the years can bring, I should have very much liked to continue my work. Placed at the heart of the parliament of my country, I had felt that I was working with far more authority and effectiveness. My opinions had finally become respectable, for they were those of a senator. Yet I was neither more intelligent nor more dynamic than before.

The inferior legal status of the women of Quebec compared to that of their sisters in other provinces had always shocked me deeply and so it was that I became progressively involved in a work that is not yet finished. As a French-speaking Canadian, I observed (and I still observe) the suspicions that divide the two founding peoples of Canada. Yet in this century of the conquest of space and the great advances in communications, it is essential for Canadians to understand one another. On the many occasions when I have represented my country at international gatherings, I have realized how necessary it is to bring human beings of all societies and all races closer together. The swift changes that are taking place on our planet seem to give its inhabitants a sense that they are witnessing the dawning of a new age in which, it is to be hoped, love will replace hate.

At the present moment, it is a joy to observe that in every part of Canada replacement forces are organizing. On all levels, the authorities are more concerned with the living conditions of the masses. Education, health, and employment have become matters of general interest. A greater number of citizens, it seems to me, are trying to participate actively in politics and are also keenly observing events in other countries. Are these impressions of mine justified? I dare to believe so, at least as far as the part played by women is concerned. At the time of the suffragettes, only a very few were involved, their minds open not only to their own problems but to those of society as a whole. Today women do not have to face the same difficulties as of old; they can make their influence more widely felt and they are listened to a little more, but a world in which men and women are completely equal is still far from being realized. All my life I have recommended that one must ask questions, take a position, and act upon it. So I approve, in general, of the wave of women's liberation that is spreading over the world, though I differ in opinion with some of the methods used by a few groups to attain their goals. Our case is surely not strengthened because some thousands of them throw, if not all sense of propriety to the wind, at least their bras into the fire. This somewhat frivolous aspect is even echoed in some of the discussions of our legislators. What advantage is there in trying to decide whether girls should be accepted as pages in Parliament or the legislatures and, if so, how should they be dressed? In my opinion, it is more important to stick to fundamental questions such as wage parity, equality of opportunity, and the presence of women on boards of directors, on royal commissions, and in our parliaments.

Even the few steps forward woman has taken on the road to her liberation do not prevent her from still being the prisoner of a host of prejudices. We are faced with a society that needs to cast off its old concepts of racism, violence, and snobbery. We are too afraid of abandoning old ways of looking at things–when patriotism meant obedience, middle age, wisdom, and woman, submission. The true liberation of women cannot take place without the liberation of men. Basically the women's liberation movement is not only feminist in inspiration, it is also humanist. Let men and women look at one another honestly and try together to give society a new set of values. The challenge which we, both men and women, must meet is that of living for a peaceful revolution and not dying for a revolution that would be cruel and, ultimately, illusory.

Notes

CHAPTER 1

1. Abbé C. Tanguay, *Dictionnaire généalogique des familles canadiennes*, Vol. 1, p. 415.
2. P. Archange Godbout, *Nos Ancêtres du XVIIième siècle*, p. 319.
3. Abbé C. Tanguay, *op. cit.*, p. 59.
4. Léon Gérin, *L'Habitant de Saint-Justin, Mémoires de la Société royale du Canada*, 2nd series, Vol. IV, May, 1889, p. 139. Léon Gérin was the first to write monographs on individual French-Canadian families and parishes.
5. *Ibid*, p. 216.

CHAPTER 2

1. L.-O. David, *Mes Contemporains*, Montreal, Les Imprimeurs Eusèbe Sénécal et Fils, 1894.
2. *Saturday Night*, November 26, 1910.
3. Mme Francoeur, *Trente Ans, rue Saint-François Xavier et ailleurs*, p. 8.
4. *Ibid*, p. 7.
5. *Ibid*, p. 8.
6. *Ibid*, p. 12.
7. He did not obtain the charter until June, 1911.
8. The grandson of Louis-Joseph Papineau, Bourassa was born in Montreal on September 1, 1868. In 1910, he founded the celebrated newspaper, *Le Devoir*. An impressive, orator, he was elected to the House of Commons on several occasions. Though an anti-imperialist and strong Quebec nationalist, Bourassa was never a separatist.
9. *Le Pays*, May 31, 1913.
10. *La Patrie*, June 18, 1918.
11. The allusions are to the first Canadian warship, *Niobe*, and to the defeat of the Laurier government in a by-election in the Drummond-Arthabaska riding in 1910. This defeat at the polls foreshadowed the final defeat of his government in 1911.

CHAPTER 4

1. Léonce Boivin, *Dans Nos Montagnes*, p. 181.

CHAPTER 5

1. L.-O. David, *Les Deux Papineau*, Montreal, Les Imprimeurs Eusèbe Sénécal et Fils, 1896, pp. 27-28.
2. *League of Women's Rights, Minute Books*, entries for January 16 and 19, 1922.
3. *La Sphère féminine* (1937-38), p. 48.
4. Catherine Lyle Cleverdon, *The Woman Suffrage Movement in Canada*, Toronto, University of Toronto Press, 1950, pp. 146-147.
5. *Ibid*, pp. 146-155.

CHAPTER 7

1. T.-D. Bouchard, *Mémoires*, Montreal, Beauchemin, 1960, p. 147.

CHAPTER 8

1. *Le Devoir*, March 23, 1940.
2. *Le Devoir*, April 12, 1940.

CHAPTER 9

1. *Hansard*, September 8, 1939, p. 25.
2. Robert Rumilly, *Bourassa*, p. 785.

CHAPTER 11

1. *Le Devoir*, October 20, 1943.
2. *Ibid.*
3. M. G. Ballantyne, "The Church and the CCF," *The Commonwealth*, March 3, 1944. See also Walter D. Young, *The Anatomy of a Party*, Toronto, University of Toronto Press, 1969, p. 212.

CHAPTER 12

1. Perrault Casgrain was the only member of the Cabinet who came to speak in my favour when I was running as an Independent Liberal candidate in Charlevoix.
2. The use of imposters to vote in the name of others.
3. Walter D. Young, *The Anatomy of a Party*, Toronto, University of Toronto Press, 1969.
4. Stanley Knowles, *The New Party*, Toronto, McClelland and Stewart, 1961, pp. 19-20.

CHAPTER 14

1. Lotta Dempsey, Mrs. J. Davis, Helen Tucker, Gaby Roblins, June Callwood, and Senators Hodges, Inman, Irving, and Quart.
2. Mrs. Pearson resigned in 1962 when the Voice of Women began to be described by the press as a communist organization.
3. *Le Devoir*, May 22, 1962.
4. *Le Devoir*, May 1, 1962.
5. Quoted in *La Presse*, March 6, 1963.
6. *Le Devoir*, January 14, 1963.
7. *Cité Libre*, April 1963.
8. "Women Strike for Peace," a group of American women having the same aim as "Voice of Women."
9. *Le Devoir*, October 7, 1965.

CHAPTER 15

1. Frédéric Girard, "La Petite Institutrice," from *Notre Petite Feuille*, Bulletin of ACIR, Vol. 1, No. 2 (1937), p. 3.
2. *Institutrice rurale*—Manifesto published by the Association des Institutrices rurales de la Province de Québec, FCIR archives, February 19, 1937.